Now You Know Tungsten™ E

by Rick Overton
and David Hayward

palmOne Press
palmOne, Inc.

Now You Know Tungsten E
by Rick Overton and David Hayward
© 2004 palmOne, Inc. All rights reserved.

For more information on this book, and the products, services, and techniques discussed within its pages, see www. palmOne.com.

This palmOne Press book is published in association with Peachpit Press, 1249 Eighth Street, Berkeley, CA 94710; (510) 524 -2178, (510) 524-2221 (fax); www.peachpit.com. To report errors, please send a note to errata@peachpit. com. Peachpit Press is a division of Pearson Education.

ISBN 0 - 321- 33030-7

9 8 7 6 5 4 3 2 1

Printed and bound in the United States of America.

Acknowledgments

Customers tell us they love our handhelds but feel like they're only scratching the surface of what can be done. *Now You Know Tungsten E* begins where that handheld's manual ends. This is a source book and an idea book, and the tips and techniques within have been customized expressly for the Tungsten E handheld.

The degree to which this book succeeds is due to the hard work of the many people listed here. Special thanks, however, must go to Arthur Manzi of palmOne, Inc. for his careful eye, thorough readings, and the many tips and suggestions he offered for improving this book.

Rose G. Rodd, Director, palmOne Press
Patrick Ames, editor in chief

palmOne, Inc.
Melissa Cha
Arleene Chua
Duane Cowgill
Leora Gordon
Scott Hancock
Joel Ingulsrud
Andrea Johnson
Robert Levin
Arthur Manzi
Page Murray
Eric Powers
Jim Schwabe
Ken Wirt

Writing & editorial
Overton Hayward Group

Representation
BookVirtual Corporation

Published in association with
Peachpit Press

Printed in the USA by
Wallace Moore

About This Book

Contents

Get Connected

Get Going

Get Media

Get Cool Stuff

Now you know

All of your applications live on the Home screen. To see all of them, make sure All is displayed in the right-hand corner.

This pocket guide is designed to be used side-by-side with your handheld. It's easy to read, and it's full of tips. Skip around to find the tips that suit your needs, or walk through the chapters in order. Practice as you go and watch your skills improve.

Do stuff fast

To save space, this book uses shorthand steps like "select **Home** > **Prefs** > **Buttons**." Translation: Go to the Home screen, tap the Prefs icon, and then tap Buttons. Steps might include entering info, opening a menu, or tapping an entry, a button, or any screen element.

Bold means "tap this"

Throughout this book, **bold** text indicates something you should tap or select.

Have you done this yet?

1 Followed the instructions that came in the box to charge and set up your handheld?

2 Inserted the installation CD, installed Palm® Desktop software, and synchronized?

3 Taken the Quick Tour from your handheld's Home screen?

4 Opened Palm Desktop on your computer and reviewed the Getting Started guide?

Tungsten™ E

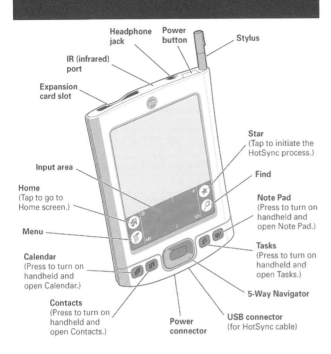

Headphone jack

Power button

Stylus

IR (infrared) port

Expansion card slot

Star
(Tap to initiate the HotSync process.)

Input area

Find

Home
(Tap to go to Home screen.)

Note Pad
(Press to turn on handheld and open Note Pad.)

Menu

Tasks
(Press to turn on handheld and open Tasks.)

Calendar
(Press to turn on handheld and open Calendar.)

5-Way Navigator

Contacts
(Press to turn on handheld and open Contacts.)

Power connector

USB connector
(for HotSync cable)

Icons to look for

Palm Desktop   Palm Desktop

Icons in the margins help you find the items discussed on the pages. All icons refer to your handheld except for the two shown above: Palm Desktop for Windows (left) and for Macintosh (right).

Marginalia

You'll find useful bits of information in the margins of every page – icons, places to go, tips and techniques, facts, and the occasional personal story.

Does this book replace my manual?

Now You Know Tungsten E goes beyond the standard documentation to delve into all the things you can do with your handheld. Along the way, it highlights key techniques that are also discussed in the Handbook, but it shouldn't be considered a substitute. See the next page to learn how to get your Tungsten E Handbook.

Flipping through

The top of every left-hand page has a header that shows the section name, followed by an arrow and the chapter number and name. Use the headers to quickly find features you're curious about.

Learn by doing

Turn the page and you move on to a new topic. Because just about everything here is a tip or a technique, you can bounce around any way you want. Keep your handheld nearby and learn by doing.

Get used to writing on small things

Write in this book! Scribble notes in the margin, circle tips to try, and jot down stuff to look up later at www.palmOne.com/support.

About This Book →

Expand your know-how

Pick the info source that suits you best	Where to find it
My Handheld News and updates, info about software and accessories. It's all here, and it's all meant for your handheld only.	www.palmOne.com/us/community/myhandheld/tungsten-e
Handbook Step-by-step instructions for mastering your handheld in a searchable, easy-to-read format.	www.palmOne.com/us/support/tungstene/handbooks.html
Quick Tour Indispensable info to guide you through the first stages of getting to know your handheld. Practice writing here.	On your handheld (go to the Home screen).
Online Support Troubleshooting, answers to general questions, how to get your handheld repaired, and other guides and downloads for your Tungsten E.	www.palmOne.com/us/support/tungstene

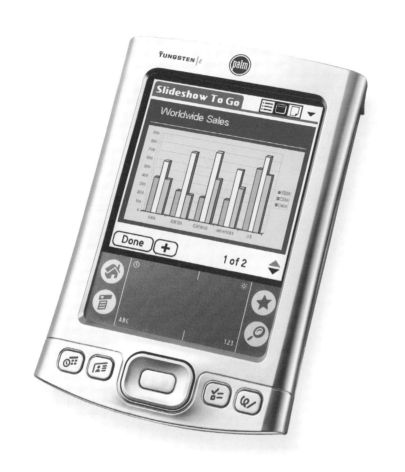

Things you can do right now

Your handheld can do all kinds of cool things. While the other chapters in this book spell out how to be productive and save time with your handheld, this chapter lists stuff you can do right now, in just a few minutes or less. Each item comes with references pointing you to other places in the book where you can learn more. Start right here.

Getting around on your handheld

Your handheld was designed to be intuitive to use. Tap with your stylus or use the navigator to move around on the screen and select items.

▶ To learn more about the stylus, see page 12.

▶ To learn more about the navigator, see page 22.

Take the Quick Tour

Your handheld comes with several built-in tools to help you use it faster and better. Quick Tour is the first application shown on the Home screen. Use it to learn handheld basics. To learn what the Home screen is all about, see page 10.

All about apps

An application (or app) is a software program. Your handheld comes with built-in applications for managing contact information, schedules, and everyday tasks. Other apps let you manage photos, play music, and even watch videos. You can buy other apps online at www.palmOne.com. For details, see pages 80 and 132.

Helpful tips

The Memos application includes some nifty tips and advice on using your handheld, in the form of actual memos. Tap the Memos icon on the Home screen and then tap any item from the list of memos.

Go home

To go to the Home screen anytime, press and hold the Center button.

Easy things to do now

Lots of easy tricks improve your ability to do what you want with your handheld. Throughout this book are tips and techniques that don't take more than a minute. Chapter 1 is full of basic tips as well as references to related parts of the book. Try the basics first, and then investigate further.

Other easy things to do now

▶ Create a new contact record for a business associate or a best friend (page 48).

▶ Learn about software that can help you at work (chapter 14).

▶ Create a contact record for yourself and make it your beamable business card (page 50).

Calculate a tip

Your handheld comes with a built-in calculator called Calc. It's great for figuring out tips, the price of stock trades, and how to divide your lottery winnings with your best friends.

When you tap **Calc** on the Home screen, your screen becomes a calculator. To calculate a 20 percent tip, enter the price of the meal, tap the multiplication button, and enter .20.

Other applications on your handheld can help you manage your money.

▶ PDAMoney (now SplashMoney) is a great place to record checking and savings account information. To learn how it works, see page 55.

▶ Track your expenses with Expense, another built-in app. Find out more on page 120.

▶ To keep track of lunch meetings, dinner dates, and coffee klatches, use Calendar. See page 57.

Make text bigger

You'll do a lot of reading on your handheld. Make text bigger and bolder in just a few seconds in Calendar, Contacts, Memos, Note Pad, or Tasks. Changing the font in one app won't affect the others.

▶ To learn about writing and entering info on your handheld, see page 37.

▶ To write a memo, see page 97.

Open any application from the Home screen that uses writing: Calendar, Contacts, Memos, or Tasks. Tap the **Menu** icon in the input area to expose the menu bar in that application. Tap or use the navigator to move to the **Options** menu. Select **Font**. Experiment with different sizes as shown to the left.

Lock the buttons

If you keep your handheld in a purse, briefcase, or jacket pocket, jostling can sometimes turn it on and drain the battery. To avoid accidentally turning on your handheld, set the Keylock preference to Automatic or Manual.

From the Home screen, select **Prefs** > **Keylock**. You'll find options for automatic or manual settings. Experiment to find a way that works well for you.

▶ To learn about the Home screen, where you can find all your handheld's applications, see page 10.

▶ To change what app opens when you press one of the buttons on your handheld, see page 33.

▶ To maximize battery life, see page 19.

▶ To set travel preferences, see page 30.

▶ To create a password for your handheld, see page 34.

Remember things now

Your handheld can remember thousands of things so you don't have to. Enter something once, and then forget about it. Various alarms, lists, records, fields, and colors help you record and manage your life and schedule. The biggest tip of all: Take the time to learn how to enter info.

Scribble a note

In Note Pad, you can write quick notes to yourself in your handwriting. Scribble phone numbers for people you just met, directions, or ideas for a weekend getaway.

From the Home screen, tap the **Note Pad** icon. A new note opens automatically. Start writing. Change the size of the pencil or erase part of the note by tapping the pencil icon.

Other ways to remember things now

▶ Set up your schedule using Calendar (page 59).

▶ Add a person's contact info to an appointment (page 58).

▶ Set a wake-up alarm with World Clock (page 31).

▶ The Tasks application is the ultimate memory machine. See chapter 10.

▶ To learn about all the things you can do with Note Pad, see chapter 12.

▶ To change the color of your pen and paper to create more attractive notes, see page 104.

▶ Add alarms to notes you create in Note Pad. See page 105.

▶ To create memos, see page 97.

▶ To add notes to tasks, appointments, and contacts, see page 44.

▶ To listen to music while you take notes, see page 112.

Remember birthdays

Contacts

To add info about a person in the Contacts application, tap his or her name, and then tap **Edit**. Scroll down by tapping the arrow in the lower-right corner or the navigator's down button until you see the **Birthday** field. Tap it, enter the date, and set a reminder for a week ahead of time.

▶ To create a contact, see page 48.

▶ To create custom fields for contact information, such as the name of a contact's spouse, see page 53.

▶ To receive contacts directly from another person's handheld, see chapter 9.

▶ To enter contact info more quickly, see page 68.

Remind yourself about an errand

The Tasks application is like a supercharged to-do list. Whether you have dry cleaning to drop off, a white paper to review, or a business trip to plan, create a task and set an alarm to stay on top of everything.

Open Tasks by tapping its icon on the Home screen. Tap **New** and enter your task. Tap **Details** and assign the task a due date. If you want a reminder, tap **Alarm**.

▶ For more about Tasks, see page 91.

▶ To learn more about writing on your handheld, see page 37.

▶ To change the alarm sound, see page 31.

▶ Create repeating tasks for things you do regularly, like reviewing weekly sales data or tracking your favorite stocks. See page 94.

Enhance what you can do now

Your handheld is a great tool by itself, but it becomes much more useful – and more fun – when it's teamed up with your PC. Learn how to use Palm® Desktop software and synchronize your handheld with your computer. After you complete the setup process spelled out in the *Read This First* guide that came with your handheld, you'll have a Palm Desktop icon on your computer's desktop (PC, below left; Mac, below right) They open Palm Desktop, an application that lets you make changes with your computer and then sync them to your handheld.

Palm Desktop

Palm Desktop

Synchronize your handheld and PC

Your handheld makes your life easier because it holds a ton of info – and shares that info with your computer. To make your handheld talk to your computer, you need to synchronize them. This is also known as a sync or the HotSync® process. To sync your

handheld to your computer, use the USB cable that came in the package. Turn both devices on. Tap the Star icon. (You might also need to tap the HotSync icon that appears.) When the process is finished, you'll see "HotSync operation complete" on your handheld screen.

Install the essential applications included on your CD

Your handheld comes with some great built-in applications. Other apps are included on the installation CD that came with your handheld.

If you have a PC...

Put the CD into your computer. When the Discover Your Handheld screen appears, click **Install Essential Software**. Click a title for a detailed description. Click **Install** for the ones you want. When you finish making all your choices, synchronize your handheld and your PC and then look for the icons on the Home screen.

If you have a Mac...

Open Palm Desktop and then insert the CD. Go to the **HotSync** menu and select **Install Handheld Files**. Click **Add to List**. Open the CD from the Add to List window, and then choose the applications you want to transfer to your handheld. When you finish, synchronize your handheld and your Mac.

Here's how Palm Desktop looks on your PC.

Here's how Palm Desktop looks on your Mac.

▶ Palm Desktop gives you a place to back up all the information that's on your handheld. To make it work, you need to learn how to sync. For sync basics, see chapter 8.

▶ To learn how to use Palm Desktop to better manage information and your life, see chapter 7.

▶ Learn how to load and edit Microsoft Excel, Word, and PowerPoint files on your handheld with the Documents To Go application. It's included on the Installation CD. You can also create new documents on your handheld, sync them to your PC, and continue working on them. See page 128.

▶ Your handheld can also play back music, audio books, and other audio in MP3 format. Use your installation CD to install RealOne® Player for free. You need an expansion card (sold separately) to store MP3s for playback on your handheld. Other audio applications are available at www.palmOne.com.

Fun things to do right now

Download a game (Windows)

The Internet is full of games you can download for free or for a few bucks. Go to www.palmone.com/software and browse the games until you find one you like that offers a free trial. After you download it, open Palm® Desktop software and click the **Quick Install** icon. Add the new game and sync to copy it to your handheld.

► To find out more about adding applications like games, see page 82.

► To find out about other software you can download, see page 154.

► To beam a game to a friend, see page 91.

View photos

You can sync photos from your computer onto your handheld and then view and arrange them. Bring a complete photo album along when you travel, or use it for business product shots or staff pictures. If your digital camera uses SD cards, put one into the card slot of your handheld, and presto! You have an instant photo viewer. Your installation CD includes Palm® Photos for free.

► Be sure to install Kinoma from Software Essentials, too, so you can watch video that's been converted to fit your handheld screen.

► Photos has a neat slide show feature. To create your own slide shows, see Chapter 13.

► To listen to music on your handheld while watching your slide show, see chapter 13.

► An expansion card can hold several hundred photos. See pages 16 and 107 for more info.

Get Started → Chapter 2 →

Things you really need to know

What you learn in this chapter will apply throughout the book, giving you a head start toward getting the most out of your handheld. If you're not familiar with the controls on your handheld, see page xi or take the Quick Tour on the Home screen.

In this chapter

▶ All about the Home screen

▶ Use the navigator

▶ Add memory and install applications

▶ Make your battery last longer

▶ What to do if your screen freezes

How your handheld is different from your PC

No need to save

Ever lose important information on your computer? One great thing about your handheld is that you don't need to save. You just enter info and it stays put. Because everything you enter is saved automatically, you can focus on more important things.

No need to quit

Applications on your handheld know that when you've moved to something else, you've quit for the time being. When you finish putting in new info, just go back to the Home screen by tapping the **Home** icon on the left side of the writing area. When you return to that application, it will be exactly as you left it.

Taps, not clicks

When you work with a handheld, clicks become taps. Tap with the stylus provided. Create info with taps, and then use the navigator to find the info you've created.

▶ For more about tapping, see page 12.

▶ To learn about the navigator, see page 22.

The Home screen

The Home screen is your center of operations, the equivalent of the desktop on your PC. Here you can view your applications, sort them by category, and open them. Learning your way around the Home screen will help you master everything else.

Cut through screen clutter
A few simple tips make the Home screen easier to use

Scrolling

If there are more icons than fit on your Home screen, scroll to the top or bottom using the scroll bar on the right, or press up and down on the navigator. A quicker way to get to an application with an icon that's not currently shown is to write the first letter of the application's name in the input area. Then tap the application to open it, or press the navigator's center button.

View by list

Large icons on your Home screen take up lots of space. For a more efficient view, select **Menu** > **Options** > **Preferences** on the Home screen. Here you can choose the icon view or the list view, which shows you more applications at once.

Use categories

The categories in the upper-right corner of the Home screen give you a

powerful way to organize your applications. To assign a category to an application in the Home screen, tap the upper-left corner of the screen and select **Category** from the **App** menu.

Edit categories

To create new categories or edit existing ones, tap the upper-right corner of the Home screen and select **Edit Categories**.

▶ For more about categories, see page 24.

Application categories
Organize your apps for speedy access

1 Tap the upper-right corner to display the Home screen's default categories. Select **Edit Categories**.

2 You can now add new categories, delete them, or rename existing categories.

3 From the Home screen, tap the Menu icon to the left of the writing area. Select **Category** to assign to each application one of your new category names.

Pick up where you left off

If you're interrupted in the middle of a task or activity, you can simply turn your handheld off. When you turn it on again using the power button, your handheld takes you right back to where you left off.

Retrieve info fast

Need to refer back to directions on your handheld while you're driving? If your handheld has turned itself off, bring up the last screen you viewed just by pressing the power button. It's that simple.

Icon to look for

Home

Go back Home

If you ever get lost or want to start over, tap the house icon to the left of the writing area, just below the screen. Alternatively, hold the navigator's center button down for a couple of seconds.

Start from Home

If you need to switch to an application that you can't open with one of the four application buttons along the base of your handheld, you must go to the Home screen and tap its icon.

Open applications fast

When your handheld is turned off, pressing one of the application buttons opens the app – you don't have to press the power button. (The icons around the writing area will not turn your handheld on.) If your handheld is on, tap the **Home** icon, and then tap an application icon.

Toggle categories

Tap the Home icon repeatedly to toggle between categories.

The screen and stylus

Your handheld's stylus and touch-sensitive screen are the two most basic tools you use to get stuff done (and have fun) on your handheld. Take good care of them and you'll keep your handheld happy.

Go to

▶ To master Graffiti® 2 writing, see chapter 4.

▶ To quickly access menus, see page 15.

Hands-on advice

Even though your fingernail can work as a stylus, it eventually will scratch the screen. Use the navigator if your stylus isn't handy.

Protect screens

A small investment in a protective case can protect your screen from the scratches and nicks of everyday use. For info on cases, see page 136.

Tapping basics

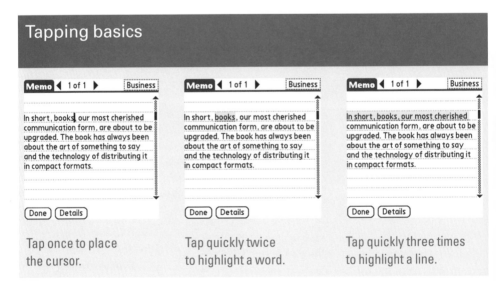

Tap once to place the cursor.

Tap quickly twice to highlight a word.

Tap quickly three times to highlight a line.

Protect your screen

Screen protectors

Screen protectors protect your handheld's screen from scratches and accidental marks. They also reduce glare and reflection, a nice benefit for use in bright daylight. You simply cut them out and apply them over the screen. Choose from a variety of styles at www.palmOne.com/store.

Care and cleaning

Every month or so, wipe your screen with a soft, clean cloth dampened with a diluted solution of window cleaner and water. You don't need much. Don't "shine" fingerprints off with your sleeve or pant leg, or you might scratch the surface. Change your screen protector once a month, or twice a month under heavy usage.

Avoid sharp objects

Never use a sharp object as a stylus, including open pens, tacks, and paper clips, and be careful of keys and coins when you're keeping your handheld in your pants pocket or purse.

Take along an extra stylus

Losing your stylus can slow you down. Get a replacement stylus to carry around, even one that fits on your key chain or comes with a built-in laser pointer. For details, see page 140.

Carrying your stylus

Some stylus models fit directly in your handheld's slot, but others don't. Don't try to jam a stylus in if it doesn't fit perfectly. Instead, consider buying a case that can hold all of your accessories, such as an expansion card and extra stylus, as well credit cards and business cards.

Homemade protection

An inexpensive way to avoid scratching the writing area is to cover it with a piece of transparent tape. Some people also cut up transparency sheets to use as screen protectors. But you'll get more reliable protection by making a tiny investment in a pack of screen protectors.

If the stylus doesn't work

When you first started using your handheld, you were asked to fine-tune the screen by tapping on targets. If your taps ever seem imprecise, select **Home** > **Prefs** > **Digitizer** and tap the bull's-eyes. This recalibrates your handheld.

How the screen works

Your screen is a sandwich of two sheets of conductive material separated by small "spacer" balls. When you tap, the screen measures the tap on horizontal and vertical axes. Over time, weather and other factors cause slight changes to the electronics. That's why you need to recalibrate occasionally with the Digitizer.

Menus and commands

The command bar

The command bar pops up when you make a command stroke. In the input area, make the command stroke by dragging the stylus from the lower left to upper right. A toolbar (the command bar, pictured above) appears for a few seconds at the bottom of the screen. Tap the icon to complete the command.

Three ways to use commands

▶ Tap the upper-left corner of the screen.

▶ Tap the **Menu** icon.

▶ Write the command stroke and letter.

Your handheld's menus are in a familiar place, along the top of the screen, but they don't become visible until you tap the upper-left corner of the screen. You can also open the menus in any app by tapping the Menu icon, located at the lower-left of the writing area. Commands are faster ways of calling up a menu action.

Create a new task with commands

1 Open **Tasks**, tap **New** to create a new task, and write /ı (for Look Up).

2 Your Contacts address book opens. Select any name and tap **Add**.

3 The name is automatically pasted into your new task with the first phone number listed.

4 Attach a note with more detail about why you should call this person by writing /a.

5 You've just created a task. Tap **Details** to set the due date and priority level.

Using commands
Commands are an easy way to activate the menus

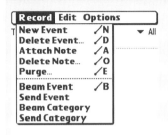

To quickly see menus, tap the **Menu** icon. Menus appear at the top of the screen, just like on your computer. If a menu item has a command, you'll see it to the right of the item.

From the menu, tap the command, or in the writing area, write a slash followed by a letter.

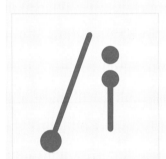

With the Home screen showing, try writing /i to execute the Info command.

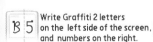
Write Graffiti 2 letters on the left side of the screen, and numbers on the right.

Note that some screens, such as this one, don't have menus.

Icon to look for

Menu

Frequently used commands

/b Beam item
/c Copy
/d Delete
/f Font
/g Graffiti 2 writing help
/i Info
/k Keyboard
/n New item
/p Paste
/s Select all
/u Undo

String together commands

Once you get the hang of menu commands, you can execute a string of them fast. For example, if you're in a memo and you write /s /c /n /p, you select all the text, copy it, create a new memo, and paste the text into that new memo.

Go to

► To learn how menus work in specific apps, check out chapters 5, 6, 10, 11, and 12.

Expansion cards

Expansion cards are about the size of a postage stamp. They slide into the top of your handheld and expand what it can do. Some add memory so that you can carry more music, photos, videos, or e-books. Other cards add functionality, such as games, dictionaries, and applications. See www.palmOne.com for a list of cards available for your handheld.

Real Life
Memory cards

 Ed uses an expansion card to carry music, which he listens to until he's tired of the songs. When he's ready to copy a new batch of music to the card, he chooses **Home** > **Card Info** > **Card** > **Format Card**, which erases the card completely. It's much faster than using the Delete menu in the Home screen.

Formatting and renaming

Formatting a card is a quick way to erase everything it contains (see "Real Life," above). When you rename a card by selecting **Home** > **Card Info** > **Card** > **Rename Card** (or writing /r), no information is lost.

How expansion cards work

Applications recognize content

When you insert an expansion card, your handheld responds based on the contents of the card and the application that's running. For example, if RealOne® Player is running and you insert a card that contains MP3 files, the songs appear on your playlist.

Share info with expansion cards

Expansion cards can easily be swapped between handhelds. Push to release one and share it with your friends. Or copy photos from your vacation or your favorite new song directly from your handheld to a friend's expansion card.

Using expansion cards

Push to insert, push to release

The *push-push* mechanism of the expansion slot works much like some cabinet doors: You push it to insert the card, and push it in again to release.

Don't force it

Don't force the card or you could damage the expansion card slot; your handheld makes a sound when you successfully insert a card.

Insert anytime

You can insert and eject expansion cards anytime the card isn't in use.

Icon to look for

Card Info

Real Life
Memory cards

Walter is a realtor who shares his office's digital camera with other agents. Rushing out of town to meet a home buyer, he grabs one of the camera's memory expansion cards, inserts it in his handheld, and shows the buyer images of homes on the market.

Supported formats

Your handheld supports the SD™ and MultiMediaCard™ formats. Both SD and MultiMediaCard types are read/write storage cards that range in size from 64MB to 1GB. Sony Memory Stick storage media and CompactFlash expansion cards are not compatible.

The dummy card

A plastic dummy card is shipped in the expansion card slot. It's not a real card, and it's in there to protect the slot. Whenever you're not using an expansion card, insert the dummy card to keep dust and other foreign material out of the slot.

How to lock and unlock an SD card

SD expansion cards have a tiny tab on the side. The label of the card tells you where to position the tab to lock the card. When a card is locked, its contents can't be changed.

Go to

▶ To learn more about expansion-card types and sizes, see page 138.

Get Started → Chapter 2 → Things you really need to know →

About the battery

Your handheld's battery should handle heavy use over the course of a day if you recharge it with the power adapter every night. There are plenty of ways to extend battery life, including changing your settings so the battery does less work. Items such as games, music, and video clips consume battery power faster than other apps.

Prevent accidental power drains

To keep your handheld from accidentally turning on and draining the battery, lock the keys. Go to **Home** > **Prefs** > **Keylock**.

Verify charge status

Make sure your handheld is properly connected to the power source when you're charging your handheld. Turn your handheld on and go to the Home screen. The lightning bolt on the battery icon tells you that your battery is being charged.

Responding to battery alerts

Sync first, then recharge

When a low-battery alert appears on the screen, it's best to back up your information with a sync, and then connect your handheld to a power source. If no power source is available, turn it off until you can charge.

Recharge as soon as possible

If the battery drains to the point that your handheld doesn't operate, it stores your information for up to a week. There's enough energy left in the battery to keep the info, but not enough to turn on your handheld. Be careful: If you leave the device uncharged for an extended period of time, you might lose all your info. If that happens, sync to get the info back.

Charge your handheld

Charge it fully

Straight out of the box, your Tungsten® E handheld needs about three hours to fully charge. After that, charging it for just 15 or 30 minutes a day will keep it powered up for light usage.

Charge regularly

Your handheld automatically shuts down when the battery is running low. For worry-free use, get in the habit of charging your handheld daily, like many people do with their mobile phones. The best practice is to routinely plug it in at night and unplug in the morning.

You can't overcharge it

You can't overcharge your handheld's battery. When the battery is full, the current is turned off.

Work while charging

You can make your handheld stay on while you're charging it, even if you leave it untouched. From the **Home** screen, select **Prefs** > **Power** and select **On** from the **On while Charging** pick list.

Bring your power adapter on the road

If you're traveling for more than a few days, take a power cord or the Travel Charger Kit, available at www.palmOne.com.

Emergency charging

When your handheld is hooked up to your computer – to sync, for example – your computer may slowly recharge the battery over the USB cable. This can serve as an emergency solution when you're traveling without a charger and need a small boost. But note that a full charge can take many hours, depending on your computer. Your handheld must be turned off while you do a trickle-charge.

Icon to look for

Check your charge

The battery icon at the top of the Home screen shows how much power you have left. A lightning bolt means the handheld is being charged.

Hot and cold

Don't expose your handheld to extreme temperatures. Keep it off your car's dashboard on hot days and take it inside in freezing weather. If it has been exposed to extremes, let it recover at room temperature.

Tips for longer battery life

▶ Reduce the brightness of the screen. Tap the small **Brightness** icon ( ) in the upper-right corner of the writing area.

▶ Shorten the time on the Auto-off setting. Select **Home** > **Prefs** > **Power**.

▶ Turn off Beam Receive. Select **Home** > **Prefs** > **Power**.

▶ Limit your use of expansion cards.

Reset your handheld

Not responding?

If your handheld isn't responding to your stylus, that doesn't necessarily mean it has crashed. First, try digitizing. Select **Home > Prefs > Digitizer** to recalibrate your stylus. Also make sure your handheld has a charge. You may think it's been charging when it hasn't.

Your handheld is remarkably stable, but sometimes an application, a sudden impact, or other factors can make it freeze or crash. To get back in business, you have to reset your handheld. Before you do, read these pages to learn the safest ways to do it – and how to avoid doing it in the first place. If your handheld does freeze, you'll know exactly what to do.

What to try before you reset

First steps

If your handheld seems frozen, try turning it off and on. If a particular application keeps freezing, the problem probably lies with that application. Delete it. If you use freeware or shareware, be sure to check out online reviews and reliability ratings.

Check versions

Incompatibility between different versions of applications and Palm OS® software is a common cause of crashes. On the Home screen, find version information at **App > Info > Version**. Then check with the app vendor about compatibility.

Delete new software

Some software can make your handheld crash. If your handheld keeps crashing, try deleting anything you've recently added or loaded. Go to **Home > Menu > App > Delete** to delete the app in question. Next, synchronize to delete it from your backup files.

Two types of reset

When to do it	What it does	How to do it
Soft		
Handheld appears to be frozen.	Handheld stops what it's doing and starts over. All of your information is retained.	The cap of your stylus unscrews to reveal a reset pin. Press the pin into the pinhole on the back of your handheld. If it doesn't work, try pressing it twice quickly.
Hard		
Soft resets don't work, or you want to erase all the info on your handheld.	**Warning:** All the info stored on your handheld will be erased. A hard reset also wipes out the username associated with the handheld. (But if you sync, you can restore it all. See "Get your info back," below.)	Use the pin, as with a soft reset, but press the power button at the same time. Release the pin, and when the logo screen appears, release the power button. At the warning, press up on the navigator.

Find the reset

The reset pinhole on your Tungsten E handheld is on the back, at the bottom of the serial number label. The word "RESET" is directly above the pinhole.

Paper clip

If you've changed your stylus, use the tip of an unfolded paper clip to gently press the reset button inside the hole on the back of your handheld.

Support help

Go to *www.palmOne.com/ support* for more about resets and when to perform them. Type in "reset" as the search term.

Get your info back

If you do a hard reset, all info is erased from your handheld. However, provided you've synchronized your info with your computer, that doesn't mean it's lost forever. After the hard reset, simply sync with your computer to restore all your info.

Selling your handheld?

If you sell your handheld, erase all your info by doing a hard reset. Let the new owner perform an initial sync.

The navigator

Turn your handheld on quickly

When your handheld is off, hold down the center navigator button until the Home screen appears (you'll get the clock first, then the Home screen).

Navigate Home

In most applications, you can return to the Home screen by holding down the center button.

One hand

The navigator works great when you're on the phone or drinking coffee, because it lets you do almost anything with one hand.

If all you're doing is looking up info that's already on your handheld, put away the stylus and use the navigator. It's the fastest way to zip around on your handheld.

Navigator basics

	Use the center button to turn your handheld on, highlight the first item on a screen, open and close entries, and return to the Home screen.
	Scroll a page up or down. In some applications, up and down bring up the next or previous entry.
	Scroll backward or forward through menus or entries. In some apps, left deselects a highlighted entry on a list.

☑ Chapter 2: Did you discover how to...

Instantly turn on your handheld and open Contacts when you get a phone call out of the blue?... Make your battery last throughout an international flight?... Choose an expansion card for use with your handheld's MP3 player... Safely reset a frozen handheld?... Quickly find out if you're appropriately late to a party?

Make your handheld uniquely your own

By mastering a few tricks and setting a few preferences, you can make your handheld as personal and secure as a fingerprint. This chapter shows you how to create categories that fit your way of doing things, how to find and delete stuff, and how to use the Prefs application to fully customize your handheld.

In this chapter

▶ Protect info from being deleted

▶ Find entries in a snap

▶ Use categories to organize information

▶ Make your handheld more secure

Mark your handheld

Telling one Tungsten™ E handheld from another can be difficult without looking inside it. To avoid mix-ups in meeting rooms and public places, tape your business card to the back of your handheld or its case. This also improves the odds of getting your handheld back quickly if you lose it.

Establish ownership

1 From the Home screen, tap **Prefs** and then tap **Owner**.

2 Enter your name and phone number so someone who finds your handheld can contact you.

3 Add a note saying something like, "If found, please contact me."

Set categories

Categories are groups of similar items on your handheld. Categories help you find people faster, schedule your day more effectively, and, in general, make mountains of info more manageable. Use categories in specific applications to group related information, like people in your book club, meetings with a certain client, or memos related to the same hobby.

Cycle through categories

To cycle through categories on the Home screen, tap the **Home** icon repeatedly. In Contacts, press the application button.

Manage categories

Create new categories

In most applications, the category pick list is in the upper-right corner. Tap it, select **Edit Categories**, and tap the **New** button to make your own.

Delete or rename categories

Select **Edit Categories**. Tap a category and then tap **Delete** or **Rename**. When you delete a category, its entries move to the Unfiled category.

Merge categories

To merge the contents of one category with another, simply rename one or both of them. If they have the same name, their entries are automatically merged.

Beam a category

Beam categories of contacts to another handheld

1 In Contacts, select a category from the pick list in the upper-right corner of the screen.

2 Tap the **Menu** icon. From the **Record** menu, select **Beam Category**.

To learn more about beaming with your Tungsten E handheld, see chapter 9.

Create new categories

Many applications come with preset categories like Business and Personal, but you can change them to suit your needs.

Category limit

Most applications allow a maximum of 15 custom categories.

Don't overdo it

If you create overly specific categories, they may turn out to be more trouble than they're worth. Check the contents of your categories every now and then, and consider deleting or merging categories that don't contain much.

Calendar categories

In Calendar, assign a color to each category. Events in each category will appear with that color in the various Calendar views. Tap an event and select **Details**. From the **Category** pick list, select **Edit Categories**. Tap the **Edit** button to change any category's color.

All and Unfiled

Two system-level categories, All and Unfiled, can't be altered. If you can't find something, check under the **All** category.

Go to

▶ See chapters 5, 6, 10, 11, and 12 for more ideas and tips for using categories.

Assigning categories

Categories work the same way in most applications, but how you assign them varies

Home

Write /y or tap the **Menu** icon and choose **Category**. Make a selection from the pick list for each application on the Home screen.

Calendar

To make the category list appear, go to **Options** > **Display Options**. Check the **Show Category List** box. To assign categories, select an event, tap **Details**, and choose from the **Category** pick list.

Contacts

Select any contact, tap **Edit**, and tap **Details**. Choose a category from the pick list. Or just tap the pick list in the upper-right corner.

How to delete stuff

From the Home screen, tap **Menu> Info** to see how much space is left on your handheld.

If you're a pack rat at home, you're probably going to use your handheld in much the same way. In that case, you might want to do a "spring cleaning" once in a while to save memory and reduce screen clutter. Be careful when deleting – depending on the application, it's often permanent.

Delete songs and photos

From the Home screen, you can't delete songs, photos, or videos stored on an expansion card. To delete such files, open RealOne® Player or Photos. From the Music or Photos menu, select **Delete**.

To delete apps from an expansion card

On the Home screen, from the **App** menu, select **Delete**. From the **Delete From** pick list, select **Card**.

Purge outdated events

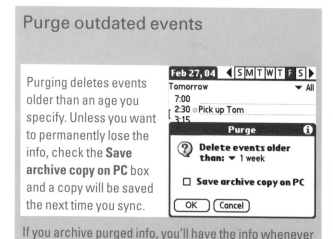

Purging deletes events older than an age you specify. Unless you want to permanently lose the info, check the **Save archive copy on PC** box and a copy will be saved the next time you sync.

If you archive purged info, you'll have the info whenever you need it.

The basics of deleting

Deleting apps

Go to **Home** > **App** >
Delete. Select the
program you want to
delete. When you delete
an application, any files
and data associated with
it are also deleted.

Freeing up memory

Eventually, you might
fill up your handheld's
internal memory. To gain
some of it back, consider
purging your Calendar and
Tasks, and delete any old,
unneeded notes, memos,
email, and names. If there
are any applications you
don't use, toss those too.
To see how much memory
your handheld has left,
select **Home** > **App** > **Info**.

Deleting entries

From inside most
applications, you can
delete individual entries
or events. Open the item
you want to delete, tap
the **Menu** icon, and
select **Record** > **Delete**.

Delete something by mistake?

If you've accidentally
deleted something, look
it up on your PC, modify
it, and then sync. Under
default conduit settings,
the most recent change
automatically transfers.
To learn more about
conduits, see page 72.

A clean slate

If you're selling your
handheld or giving it
away, erase all your info
by performing a hard reset.
See page 21.

Built-in apps

You can't delete built-in
apps like Calendar and
Contacts. You can only
delete apps that show
up in the list at **Home** >
App > **Delete**.

Retrieve archives

Archived info for each
app is stored in separate
files on your PC. Open
the application in Palm®
Desktop software, and
select **File** > **Open Archive**.
Select the archive and
click **Open**. As with your
regular info, you can copy
it, export it, and send it
to Word or Excel. Select
File > **Open Current** to
return to your current info.

Commands

/d Delete

/i Info

/e Purge

Go to

▶ To learn how to use
Palm Desktop and sync
your handheld so you
have a backup in case
you accidentally delete
something, see page 76.

How to find stuff

Icon to look for

Find

You could fit your neighborhood's phone book on your handheld, but that doesn't matter if you can't find the neighbor you want. Fortunately, your handheld has an excellent way to track down info no matter where it is.

To find...

... a contact

In the **Contacts** list view, press right on the navigator to use Look Up (see "Use the Look Up tool," next page).

... what happened during your last sync

Tap the **HotSync®** icon on the Home screen and then tap the **Log** button. On a PC, select **View Log** from the HotSync Manager menu.

... an app you just transferred

On the Home screen, look in either the **All** or the **Unfiled** category.

Search by area code

If you've forgotten someone's name but remember where the person lives, use **Find** and search by area code to track the person down.

Find in Palm Desktop software

Palm Desktop's Find function can be a fast and powerful tool. In Windows, Find is on the Edit menu. On Macs, it's on the Locate menu.

Using Find

1. Tap the **Find** icon to the right of the input area and write the text you're seeking.

2. Tap **OK**. The Find utility searches many apps and indicates where matches occur.

3. Select any of the matches to go straight to instances of the word in that application.

Use the Look Up tool
Quickly find a phone number with one hand

1 Press the **Contacts** button on the front of your handheld to go to your address book. Press right on the navigator. The Look Up boxes appear at the bottom of the screen.

2 Press up or down on the navigator to scroll through the alphabet. Press right to add a letter to your search term and narrow your search.

3 When you find the contact you want, press the center navigator button to highlight the contact. Press it again to view the contact's details.

How Find works

The Find utility searches for words that *begin* with your search terms, not ones that contain those search terms. So "ire" will find "Ireland" but not "Fire department."

Advanced Find features

To find search terms embedded in words, try the FindHack shareware utility, available online. (Make sure you get an up-to-date version.)

Real Life
Using Find

Reggie makes so many sales calls that he often forgets key details like the last time he met with a particular client. When he gets a phone call from such a client, he quickly selects the name in Contacts, taps **Find**, and scans the matches from his Calendar. Within a few seconds, he's fully up to speed. And he never has to ask, "Remind me – when did we meet?"

Tips for finding stuff

▶ Capitalization is ignored in searches.

▶ When you use the Find command within an application, it searches that application first.

▶ The more information you have in your handheld, the longer the search.

▶ Private entries, whether masked or hidden, will not appear in search results.

▶ You can't search for items stored on an expansion card.

Time and travel

Cathleen lives in a small town in the Midwest, but her consulting job repeatedly takes her to Atlanta and Phoenix. Whenever she gets off the plane, she simply selects the correct city from the primary city pick list. She always uses the alarm clock feature in World Clock and hasn't asked for a wake-up call in years.

Your handheld's World Clock application helps you keep accurate time even when you're passing through several time zones in a day. There's also a handy Alarm Clock feature with a range of alert sounds to choose from.

Clock

To check the time from any application, tap the **Clock** icon in the upper-left corner of the writing area.

Check the time

If your handheld is off, press the center button of the navigator to see the clock.

Set the time zone

To change your time zone, open World Clock. Change the top city to one in your time zone. Note that when you change time zones, your Calendar events remain scheduled at their original times.

Display foreign time formats

From the Home screen, select **Prefs** > **Formats**. Select an appropriate country. The hour and date conventions of that location are displayed. Change them if you like.

What time is it?

When your handheld is on, the current time is displayed on the Home screen and on the Agenda View of Calendar.

Change the time

From the Home screen, select **Prefs** > **Date & Time** to change your current location, set the date, and adjust the time. Change the city on the **Location** pick list, and the time changes automatically. Or, in World Clock, tap **Set Date & Time**.

Add your city to World Clock

1 Tap **World Clock** on the Home screen. Or, if your handheld is off, press the center navigator button and tap **Go to Clock**.

2 From the city pick list in the top part of the screen, select **Edit List** and tap **Add**. Select your city from the list and tap **OK**.

3 If your city doesn't appear on that list, select a city in the same time zone and tap **OK**.

4 On the **Edit Location** screen, change the name of the city, and tap **OK**.

Icons to look for

Prefs   World Clock

World Clock tips

► Select **Options** > **Alarm Preferences** to set volume controls and pick one of six different alarm sounds.

► If all you want is to see the time, select **Options** > **Display Options** and deselect **Show Multiple Locations** and **Show Date**.

Set an alarm

In World Clock, tap the box next to the alarm clock icon in the upper-right corner and the **Set Alarm** screen comes up. Select a time and tap **OK** or tap the **Alarm Off** button. Like a typical alarm clock, World Clock allows you to set an alarm only within the next 24 hours.

Go to

► To get tips on traveling with your handheld, see page 142.

Personal preferences

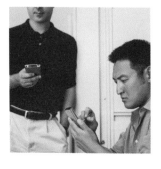

Sounds interesting

To differentiate the World Clock alarm tone from other sounds, select **World Clock** > **Menu** > **Options** > **Alarm Preferences**. To set Calendar's Alarm tone, go to **Calendar** > **Menu** > **Options** > **Preferences**.

The Prefs (or Preferences) application is where you go to make your handheld look, sound, and act just the way you want it to. Take advantage of it to customize your handheld. Do you dress in a certain way to represent your mood? Why not dress up your handheld with a different color theme? And why not replace that alarm with something less alarming?

Change your tune
The Sounds & Alerts tool in Prefs lets you adjust sound volume

Silent treatment

During a presentation or other hush-hush situation, tap **Silent** to mute your handheld. When you tap **Custom**, your previous settings are restored.

Alarm volume

Use the **Alarm Sound** pick list to set the volume of the alarm used by reminders you set for yourself. Note that this setting does not affect World Clock's alarm level.

Game volume

Some games have their own custom sounds, but most use a simple beep to accompany various actions. Adjust the volume of this beep by tapping **Game Sound**.

Change the buttons
Make buttons open whatever applications you want

1 From the Home screen, tap **Prefs**. Under Personal, tap **Buttons**. (You might have to use the scroll arrow on the right to find this option.)

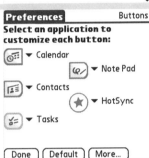

2 Tap any button name to show the pick list, and then select what you want that button to open. As you add applications to your handheld, more choices will appear.

Change your Color Theme

Select **Home > Prefs > Color Theme** to change your handheld's display conventions, either for better visibility or just for fun. For night reading, try **Midnight**. Test all of them by pressing up and down on the navigator.

When you find one you like, go back to the Home screen and test it with some of your favorite applications. By the way, changing your Color Theme has no effect on battery consumption.

Icons to look for

Prefs Alarm

Customize formats
To change the country setting and the way time, dates, numbers, and weeks are displayed, tap **Home > Prefs > Formats**.

Write on-screen
Most people write in the writing area, but you can also form letters on the screen itself. In **Prefs > General > Writing Area**, select **Write anywhere on-screen**, and form letters and numbers outside the writing area as well as within it. When this box is checked, you can also check the **Show pen strokes** box to see the strokes as you write them.

Turn off the chime
Tired of hearing that little chime every time you sync? To turn it off, go to **Home > Prefs > Sounds & Alerts** and turn **System Sound** to **Off**.

Security preferences

A sample from a Calendar Day View with two masked entries. Masked entries are hidden by gray bars.

Want your handheld to be an open book? A top-secret dossier? A combination of the two? Use a password to protect your entire handheld with Auto Lock, or to block individual entries from prying eyes. Security settings are easy to change if you find them too tight or too loose.

Security apps

Applications such as SplashID are available for purchase to help you keep track of all your passwords and credit card info. If you ever lose your purse or wallet, nothing is more helpful than a (carefully protected) handheld full of secure info.

Go to

▶ To activate your handheld's password in Palm Desktop, see page 76.

Password first

Masking or hiding a private entry doesn't protect it until you've created a password. Create a password that's familiar enough to remember without writing down, but obscure enough to foil a determined intruder.

What happened to my info?

Do you remember creating an entry that you can't find now? Maybe you marked it private, and hid it. To display hidden info, go to **Home** > **Prefs** > **Security** > **Current Privacy Level**. Tap **Show Private Records**.

Create a password

1 Go to **Home** > **Prefs** > **Security**. Tap the **Password** box. Follow the prompts.

2 Enter a hint that'll help you remember your password if you forget it.

Set your level of privacy

1 First, you must create a password. From the Home screen, tap **Prefs**, select **Security**, and enter a password and a hint.

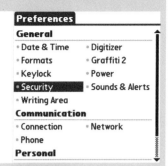

2 From the Current Privacy pick list, select Show, Mask, or Hide Private Records. Masking shows something is being hidden; hiding makes it completely invisible.

3 To apply the privacy option in Contacts, go to the **Details** dialog box for the entry and check the box marked **Private**.

Lock your handheld

Lock your handheld so others can't see any of its contents without entering its password. Select **Home** > **Prefs** > **Security** > **Auto Lock**. Lock your handheld when the power is off, at a certain time each day, or after a preset delay.

Create a hint

Create a hint when you create your password. The hint shows up in a message box when you enter your password incorrectly.

Icon to look for

Prefs

Lock entries

Protect sensitive info in any of your major applications. Within an entry, tap **Details**. (Or, in **Calendar** or **Contacts**, select **Edit** > **Details**.) Check the box marked **Private**. Note that the entry will be masked if you've chosen Mask Private Records or hidden completely if you've first chosen Hide Private Records in the Security preferences.

Security tips

▶ Never write your password in any application; instead, add a really good hint.

▶ Be careful when you hide entries. Because they don't show up at all, they're easy to forget.

Delete or change your password

To delete or change your password, select **Home** > **Prefs** > **Security.** Tap **Assigned,** enter your password, and then tap **Unassign**.

Get Started → Chapter 3 → Make your handheld uniquely your own →

Communication preferences

Real Life
Beam to phone

Horace runs a summer camp. Each spring, he likes to remind the parents of the previous year's campers to reserve spots early. Instead of entering all 30 phone numbers manually, he beams the info in his "Parents" Contacts category to his IR-enabled mobile phone.

Go to

▶ For details on communication preferences involving phones, networks, and modems, see the Tungsten E Handbook (page xii).

Communication prefs offer advanced ways to connect your handheld to your PC, or connect to a GSM-enabled phone to check your email or surf the Internet (required hardware sold separately). If you work for a company with an IT staff, ask them about the right network settings to use.

Infrared technology

The infrared (IR) technology built into your Tungsten E handheld makes it possible to send– or beam–info wirelessly to other IR-enabled devices, including many phones and computers. To learn more about what you can do with beaming, see chapter 9.

Connect to the web

With a little prep work in **Home > Prefs > Connection** and some extra software, you can connect your Tungsten E handheld to the web through your mobile phone. For step-by-step directions on making the connection, open the Tungsten E Handbook from the Help menu in Palm Desktop (see page xii).

☑ **Chapter 3: Did you discover how to...**

Enter info with a few quick commands?... Find what's-her-name's phone number?... Clear up space for a new game on an overcrowded handheld?... Use a password to protect your top-secret info?

Get Organized → Chapter 4 →

Enter info

Graffiti® 2 writing and the onscreen keyboard make it easy to enter information and capture your thoughts and ideas. You'll get the hang of writing pretty quickly, but a few tips and techniques can speed you along. Graffiti 2 writing is the system your handheld uses to translate your stylus strokes into letters, numbers, and punctuation marks. You can also type with the onscreen keyboard or buy an optional keyboard (see page 141).

In this chapter

▶ Write faster using the Graffiti 2 alphabet

▶ Save time by creating custom ShortCuts

▶ Create notes and add them to entries

The writing area

You write Graffiti 2 characters (see page 41) in the writing area–the space between the navigator and the screen. Write on the left side of the writing area for lowercase letters. Write in the middle for caps, and on the right side for numbers. Try the tip to the left to actually see your strokes as you make them.

Alternatives

Jot (www.cic.com) and TealWrite (www.tealpoint. com) are replacements for Graffiti 2 writing that use different characters.

Write on the whole screen
You don't have to limit yourself to the writing area

1 From the Home screen, select **Prefs** > **Writing Area**. Tap **On** and check **Show pen strokes**.

2 Open an application such as Memos and try writing anywhere on the screen.

3 Tap the small purple square in the lower-right corner to toggle the feature off and on.

Get Organized → Chapter 4 → Enter info →

Ways to enter info

Your handheld gives you several ways to enter info. The onscreen keyboard makes it easy to tap out words. Graffiti 2 writing may take a little practice, but it can be faster. Other methods include using a portable keyboard, receiving beamed information from another handheld, and synchronizing to transfer information from your PC.

Other input methods

Palm® Desktop software

When you need to enter lots of info at once, typing on your computer is faster than writing on your handheld. Use Palm Desktop to enter the info, and then sync to copy it to your handheld. For much more about Palm Desktop, see chapter 7.

Portable keyboards

Want to take extensive notes during a meeting, or write a letter during a flight? Wired and wireless keyboards turn your handheld into a smaller, lighter alternative to a laptop. They work like a full-size keyboard but fold up for maximum mobility. For complete details, see page 141.

Receive beamed information

When another person beams information to you from a handheld, you don't have to write at all to add important info to Contacts, Tasks, Calendar, and other applications. Don't forget that you can beam and receive entire categories, not just single entries and files. For details, see chapter 9.

The onscreen keyboard

1 Tap **ABC** in the writing area for a keyboard set up like a computer keyboard. Tap **Shift** to capitalize one letter; tap **Cap** to type in all caps.

2 Tap **123** to enter numbers and symbols. Note the international financial symbols, a handy feature for travelers.

3 Use the international keyboard to enter common international letters and symbols.

Keyboard layouts

From any application that involves writing, you can access the onscreen keyboard. Tap one of the two keyboard icons in the writing area: **ABC** or **123**.

Capitalization

In applications, the first letter of an entry or sentence is automatically capitalized and the next letters are lowercased, whether you use the writing area or the onscreen keyboard. When you end a sentence with a period, exclamation point, or question mark, the first letter of the next word is capitalized.

Blinking cursor

If you start to write and nothing shows up on the screen, tap the screen where you want your text to go. If a blinking cursor shows up, you know you can enter info.

Practice writing

The Quick Tour is the best place to start practicing your writing skills. From the Home screen, select **Quick Tour** > **Graffiti 2** and follow the prompts.

Edit typed content

When you're typing with the onscreen keyboard, you can use Graffiti 2 strokes to edit the text before entering it into the application you're using.

Go to

▶ If your stylus isn't working, see page 13.

▶ To create memos, see chapter 11.

▶ To use Note Pad to jot notes, see chapter 12.

Practice writing

Quick help

Your handheld includes an on-board help system for Graffiti 2 writing. With your stylus, make a line from the bottom of the writing area all the way to the top of the screen. Find the stroke you need, or tap the bottom-right arrows for punctuation and more.

Spaces and other characters

Make a space by drawing a short horizontal line from left to right. Erase by drawing the same line backwards. For a line return, make a slash from the upper-right to lower-left corner.

With a little practice, you'll quickly get the hang of writing letters, numbers, and punctuation.

Improve your accuracy

Watch your stylus as you write to make fewer errors.

Quick reference

Apply the Graffiti 2 stickers that came with your handheld to the inside of your handheld's cover.

Capitals and special characters

1 Write lowercase letters on the left side of the writing area and numbers on the right side. To write capital letters, use the middle of the writing area.

2 Create special characters by drawing an upward stroke, the special character, and another upward stroke.

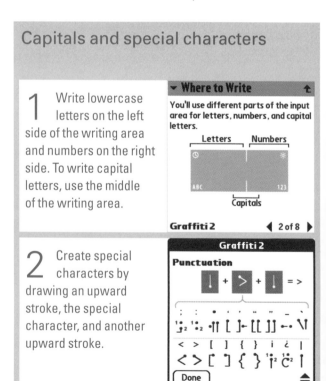

The Graffiti 2 alphabet
The heavy dots indicate the starting point for each character

Letters

Capitals

a b c d e f g h i j
k l m n o p q r s t
u v w x y z

Numbers

0 1 2 3 4 5 6 7 8 9

Punctuation

. , ' " ! & @ ? space return

Symbols

( ) / \ ~ + - * . =

Accents

/ \ ~ .. ^ °

Special characters

$ ¢ € ¥ £ ƒ TM ® © %

÷ μ ° ; : ' " " ¡

¿ · ¬ ' ‚ ^ # § ß ø

ç < > [ ] { }

Gestures

cut   copy   paste   undo   erase   tab   shortcut   shift   cmd

Get Organized → Chapter 4 → Enter info →

ShortCuts

Real Life ShortCuts

 Charlotte runs a river-rafting camp. She made custom ShortCuts to quickly enter long phrases she used to have to write out every day: "rafting this weekend" (𝓵r·f); "day-long rafting tour" (𝓵dl); "half-day expedition" (𝓵hd); and "traveling expense" (𝓵·tr).

ShortCuts let you instantly input the words, phrases, and sentences you use over and over. Enter the ShortCut symbol followed by the abbreviation, and the words appear. Your handheld comes with some preset ShortCuts, but you should create your own to take full advantage of the feature.

ShortCut length

ShortCuts can represent a maximum of 45 characters.

Use the date stamp

The date stamp is a great way to quickly record when you talked to somebody or recorded info. Use it to start notes attached to contacts (see page 44) and in Memos (see page 100).

Find by date

If you get in the habit of using the date stamp, you can quickly find info by date. Tap the **Find** icon, enter the date, and all entries from that date will show up. For more on using Find, see page 28.

Preset shortcuts

𝓵ds	Date stamp
𝓵·ts	Time stamp
𝓵d·ts	Date/time stamp
𝓵me	Meeting
𝓵br	Breakfast
𝓵lu	Lunch
𝓵di	Dinner

Create a custom ShortCut

1. Select **Home** > **Prefs** > **ShortCuts** > **New**. The ShortCut Entry dialog box appears.

2. Under ShortCut Name, write the ShortCut letters. Under ShortCut Text, write the full text.

Use a ShortCut

1 Write the ShortCut character (ℓ) in the writing area, followed by the ShortCut abbreviation for date/time stamp: dts.

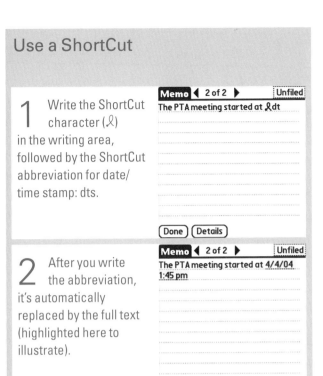

Memo ◀ 2 of 2 ▶ : Unfiled
The PTA meeting started at ℓdt

(Done) (Details)

2 After you write the abbreviation, it's automatically replaced by the full text (highlighted here to illustrate).

Memo ◀ 2 of 2 ▶ : Unfiled
The PTA meeting started at 4/4/04 1:45 pm

(Done) (Details)

Preferences   ShortCuts
    ShortCut Entry   ℹ
ShortCut Name:
ret
ShortCut Text:
return message from|

(OK) (Cancel)

When you create a new ShortCut, the letters you write on the screen after the ShortCut stroke make up the name of the ShortCut. The phrase created by the ShortCut is the ShortCut text.

Find ShortCut possibilities

Go through your entries in Calendar, Memos, and Tasks and make a list of words and phrases that show up repeatedly. Create a custom ShortCut for each of these phrases (or at least for the longest ones). You will be surprised how much time you save in the long run.

Icon to look for

Prefs

Add a space

Include a space after a word when you create a custom ShortCut so you won't have to add one after the word or phrase appears.

Assign numbers

For even shorter ShortCuts, consider using numbers (as in ℓ2 or ℓ9).

Ideas for custom ShortCuts

Here are a few examples of phrases you might want to make into ShortCuts. Note that when you create a ShortCut, you can use it in any app.

▶ Calendar: "Deadline," "Don't forget to bring"

▶ Contacts: "Vice President," "Admin. Assistant"

▶ Note Pad: "Phone number," "Meeting Notes," "Sketch of"

▶ Tasks: "Call for reservation," "Return message from," "Pick up"

Add notes to entries

Icon to look for

Note

To see whether you've attached a note to an entry, look for the icon above. Tap it to go straight to the note's contents.

The Calendar, Contacts, and Tasks applications have their own note functions that let you keep extra information attached to the entry it belongs to. These notes are an easy way to record and update important information – details, reminders, driving directions, minutes – that doesn't fit within the application's regular fields. Use your computer to cut and paste text from the web into a Palm Desktop application. Synchronize to add the info to your handheld.

Go to

To learn more about writing in specific applications, see:

▶ Memos, chapter 11

▶ Note Pad, chapter 12

▶ Contacts, chapter 5

▶ Calendar, chapter 6

▶ Tasks, chapter 10

Copy and paste info into a note

1 Highlight a word or phrase in Memos or another text-oriented application. Copy it by writing /c.

2 Go to Calendar or Contacts and tap an entry. Tap **Details**.

3 Tap the **Note** icon in the lower-right corner. Paste the copied text by writing /p.

Attach a note to a contact

1 Open Contacts and select a contact. From the **Record** menu, select **Attach Note** (/a). Or tap **Edit**, and then tap the **Note** icon.

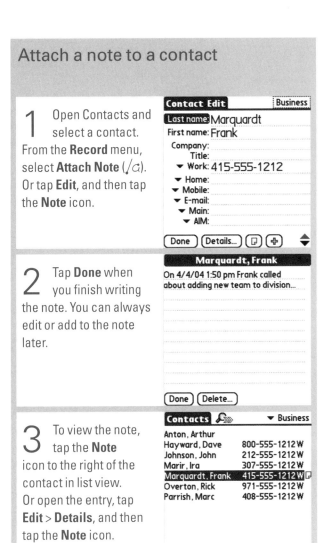

2 Tap **Done** when you finish writing the note. You can always edit or add to the note later.

3 To view the note, tap the **Note** icon to the right of the contact in list view. Or open the entry, tap **Edit** > **Details**, and then tap the **Note** icon.

Remember conversations

Use notes in Contacts to record details of conversations. A date stamp (see page 42) and a brief description might be all you need. You can always update the note later.

Travel directions

Notes are great for keeping track of travel directions. In Contacts, attach notes with driving directions for people you visit occasionally. In Calendar, attach flight numbers and itineraries to events for quick reference.

Use notes regularly

Make a habit of using notes. If you keep essential info attached to the event, contact, or task it relates to, you'll never have to search for it in drawers, notebooks, or your brain.

Notes for Tasks and Expense

In Tasks, select any entry and tap the **Note** icon to the right of **Details** to create a note. In Expense, select an entry and select **Details** > **Note**.

Track meetings

Keep a note attached to business contacts with the date you last met and a few lines to remind you what you talked about.

Record gift ideas

When a friend or family member mentions something they enjoy or want, create a note and attach it to their contact info.

Menu commands

/a Attach a note

/d Delete a note

More writing techniques

Note Pad

For pure speed, Note Pad can't be beat. Just press the Note Pad button on the lower-right corner of your handheld, and then jot down quick ideas or sketches. Return to them later and copy them into a memo, an entry note, or a record field.

Align the screen

If your writing strokes aren't producing the results you want, select **Home** > **Prefs** > **Digitizer** to recalibrate the screen. Repeat the process every few months.

The more creative you are about entering information, the more effective your handheld will be.

Use ShortCuts and notes together

Notes attached to entries and events are a great way to capture detail that you might otherwise forget. Use the date/time stamp to remember exactly when you met a person or last talked to her on the phone. Keep notes that remind you when you said you'd call or what you promised to do.

Gestures versus commands

Your handheld gives you several ways to do the same thing. You can copy and paste by tapping the menus, by writing (/c/p), or by using gestures (/⌐/ꝿ). You can use commands through the command toolbar, through the menus, or by writing. Experiment to find the methods that work best for you. To learn more about gestures, see page 41. For more about commands, see page 14.

☑ **Chapter 4: Did you discover how to...**

Write "Meet Alexandra for lunch" in a second?… Turn your handheld into an ultraportable laptop?… Attach a note to your florist's contact info to remind yourself which bouquet you ordered last time?

Get Organized → Chapter 5 →

Contacts

Contacts is the best address book you've ever had. But it's not just for keeping in touch. Use Contacts to build your network, introduce like-minded people to each other, and remind yourself of birthdays and other big events. Contacts works smoothly with other applications to make sure the things you do stay connected to the people you do them with.

Identify yourself in Contacts

In case you ever lose your handheld, make it easier for the person who finds it to find you. Create a contact with the following note as the last name: "+If found, contact [your name and phone number]." The + symbol causes the contact to rise to the top of the contact list.

Share contact info fast

At conferences, get-togethers, and other events, beam and receive contact information whenever you can. It's faster and more accurate than entering the info manually. To beam contact info, tap the contact's name, tap the **Menu** icon, and select **Record > Beam Contact** (/b).

In this chapter

▶ Replace your paper address book

▶ Create new contacts quickly

▶ Assign custom fields and unique categories

▶ Attach a note to a contact

Sync Contacts from Outlook

When you first set up your handheld with your computer, you were asked whether to use Outlook or Palm® Desktop as your computer's default info manager. You can switch to Outlook at any time. Just insert your installation CD into your computer and select **Install Microsoft Outlook Conduits**. Your handheld's contacts stay the same, but are now synchronized with the personal info manager of your choice.

Get Organized → Chapter 5 → Contacts →

Create new contacts

Don't hesitate to add incomplete contacts, even if all you have is a name and email address from a brief exchange. You never know when it'll come in handy. When it does, Contacts makes the person easy to find.

Use Palm Desktop

Palm Desktop is a great, quick way to enter contact info. Type in info on your PC and sync to your handheld when you're done.

Auto-complete

When you enter letters in the Title, Company, City, and State fields, a match will appear if one of your contacts has a similar field name. When the word you want appears, tap the next field. (Note that auto-complete doesn't work if you're using the onscreen keyboard.)

Enter info

Order is important

If a contact has several phone numbers, the first one you enter becomes the main phone number. When you first open Contacts, that's the number that appears in list view. To see additional numbers, tap the contact.

Change the order

Have a friend who prefers to be called on his cell phone? Customize his info to make that number appear in list view. Select the contact, tap **Edit** > **Details**, and pick the number from **Show in List**.

Duplicate to save time

To quickly add people who work in the same office or live together, use Duplicate Contact to save time. Go to the contact you want to duplicate and select **Duplicate Contact** from the menu. The information appears in the Contact Edit mode so you can edit fields that are unique, such as the name, job title, email, and phone extension.

Enter addresses

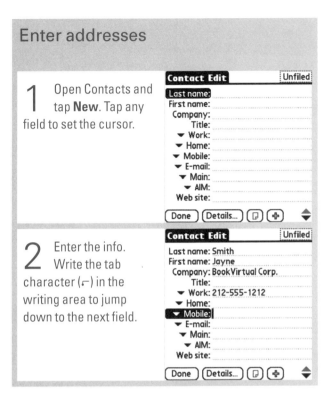

1 Open Contacts and tap **New**. Tap any field to set the cursor.

2 Enter the info. Write the tab character (⌐) in the writing area to jump down to the next field.

Add fields

If you want to add an instant-messaging address or you just run out of room in a contact, open the contact and tap **Edit**. Tap the blue **+** icon and pick the type of field to add.

Find contacts

Use Look Up, at the bottom of list view, to find a contact fast. Or use Find to search by area code.

Auto caps

In Contacts, the first word in all fields except numeric and email fields is automatically capitalized.

Type your entries

Don't forget your onscreen keyboard! Filling in some fields with handwriting can be frustrating, especially for email addresses and URLs, which require special characters. Write (⁄k) to quickly call up the keyboard. To get symbols such as @, tap the **123** box at the bottom of the keyboard screen (see page 39).

Icon to look for

Contacts

Address fields

Want to keep track of your sister's home, business, and beach house addresses? Each contact can have up to three addresses. Designate an address as work (W), home (H), or other (O). By default, the first address is designated as work (W). To add another address for a contact, tap the blue **+** icon at the bottom of the screen and select **Address**.

Beam contacts

Beam the info for one of your contacts by selecting **Record** > **Beam Contact** or by using the beaming command (⁄b). To beam an entire category, select it from the pick list at the upper right and select **Record** > **Beam Category**.

Go to

▶ For tips about writing, see page 40.

▶ To learn commands, see page 14.

Contacts menus

Contacts 🖋️	▼ Book Group
C., Willa	555-1212 W
D., Joan	555-1212 H
E., Jane	555-1212 W
E., Ralph	555-1212 H
J., James	555-1212 W
M., Janet	555-1212 M
R., Richard	555-1212 M
W., Molly	555-1212 H

Look Up: _____ (New)

Contacts is so handy that you might quickly find your address book growing like crazy. Use the menus to take control so the names and numbers you need are easy to find.

Password protection

If you want to keep track of sensitive information like your brokerage account number or your children's social security numbers, go to **Home** > **Prefs** > **Security** to mask or hide contacts with a password. See page 34.

Use multiple cards

Create multiple business cards if you don't want to share your home phone number with business contacts, or your work address with new friends. Remember to reset which card is your business card before you beam.

Create your business card

Create a business card with all your contact info. Tap the **Menu** icon and select **Record** > **Select Business Card**.

Share your business card

Press and hold the **Contacts** button to beam your business card. It's the quickest way to swap info when you're networking.

Delete a contact

1	From the list view, tap any entry to display it. Then tap the **Menu** icon.
2	Select **Delete Contact** from the **Record** menu, or write /d in the Graffiti® 2 writing area.
3	Don't uncheck the **Save archive copy on PC** box unless you're sure you'll never need the info.
4	Tap OK. Sync to save the archive copy.

Contacts menus

Record (list view)

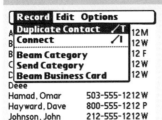

For people at the same company, use **Duplicate Contact** to duplicate all the contact info, and then just change the name, phone, and email.

Options (list view)

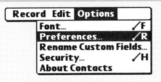

You can change the font in list view without affecting the font in entry view (**Options > Font**). In **Preferences**, check the **Remember Last Category** box to make Contacts show the last category you selected when you open the application again.

Record (entry view)

Delete, duplicate, and beam a contact from this view. If you have connectivity software, you'll see Send Contact and Connect (shown), which open other applications such as email. You can attach or delete a note from this view as well as from the entry view.

Emergency contacts

In a crisis, you don't have time to sort through all your contact information. Create a category called "Emergencies" to keep phone numbers for fire, police, the veterinarian, and baby-sitters.

Customize contact info

If you want to remember a contact's spouse's name or a client's favorite restaurant, create a custom field in Contacts. Select **Menu > Options > Rename Custom Fields**.

Remember birthdays

Instead of entering birthdays in Calendar, use Contacts. Open Contacts, tap **Edit**, scroll down, and tap **Birthday**. Contacts automatically enters it in Calendar.

Using Contacts

Sync to save time

Create contacts in Outlook or Palm Desktop software, and then sync. You'll save time and speed up the entry process.

Sync to back up

Whether you sync with Outlook or Palm Desktop software, your addresses and phone numbers are backed up, creating a safety net for some of your most important info.

Attach notes

Attach a note with directions to a friend's house. Select the contact, tap **Edit**, and tap the **Note** icon. The note stays attached until you delete it. To learn more about using notes, see page 44.

Contacts can record and track all the info you need about the people you work with, go out with, and even those you see for a few minutes every holiday season. Speedy access is why Contacts is such a powerful application and why you should examine these pages.

Look up contacts with the navigator

Contacts	▼ Business
DeBeers, Conor	707-555-1212 W
Hamad, Omar	503-555-1212 W
Hayward, Dave	800-555-1212 P
Johnson, John	212-555-1212 W
Marir, Ira	307-555-1212 W
Marquardt, Frank	415-555-1212 W
Moskal, Alison	415-555-1212 O
Overton, Rick	971-555-1212 W
Parrish, Marc	408-555-1212 W
Peel, Winifred	+44 989 6756 8765 W
Smith, Oscar	206-555-1212 W

Look Up: **H A M**

In the Contacts list view, press right on the navigator to display the letter boxes. Press up or down to scroll through the alphabet, and press right to select the next box. When the contact appears onscreen, press the center button. Scroll to the name you want, and press center to open the contact info.

Create custom fields

1 Select **Options** >
Rename Custom Fields. Tap any of the nine fields and enter a new name.

Rename Custom Fields ℹ
To rename any custom field below, enter a new name:

dog's name	Custom 5
fave flower	Custom 6
Xmas crd lst?	Custom 7
Custom 4	Custom 8
	Custom 9

(OK) (Cancel)

2 Use custom fields any way you like. Remember that they appear in all contacts, not just an individual category.

Contact Edit   Business
- ▾ Addr(W):
  - City: Sussex
  - State:
  - Zip Code:
  - Country: Britain
  - Birthday: -Tap to add -
- dog's name:
- fave flower: Petunia
- **Xmas crd lst?** Yes
- Custom 4:

(Done) (Details...) (🗋) (✛)   ⬍

Use categories

Contacts has five default categories: All, Business, Personal, QuickList, and Unfiled. Tap the pick list in the upper-right corner to view categories. From the list, select **Edit Categories** to create, rename, or delete categories.

Scroll categories

Categories make it easier to sort Contacts with one hand. Make a category for a city you're visiting, or for people you expect to see at a party. When you need fast info, just press the Contacts button to scroll through the categories.

Category maximum

You can have as many as 15 Contacts categories, and each contact can be assigned to only one category. Select the **All** category to see all your contacts at once.

Sample categories for different users

Parent	College Student	Part-time coach
Other parents	Study group	Team members
Baby-sitters	Friends	Other coaches
Home maintenance	Family	Umpires
Emergency	Hiking Club	Doctors

More Contacts techniques

After you've used your handheld for a while, go back through the Contacts menus and take a second look at this chapter. You might learn something useful that you missed the first time around.

Archive contacts when you delete

To keep a backup of a contact you're deleting from your handheld, keep the **Save archive copy on PC** box checked.

Merge categories

If you have too many categories, change the name of one to the name of one that already exists. The contacts will merge into that category. If you delete a category, all the contacts in it are assigned to the Unfiled category, meaning you'll have to refile them all.

Go international

Accurate information for international contacts often requires special characters. To enter foreign characters in an application, tap **ABC** in the writing area to call up the onscreen keyboard. Then tap **Int'l**. Find financial symbols such as the Euro sign by tapping **123**.

☑ **Chapter 5: Did you discover how to...**

Remember Aunt Karen's birthday, for the first time since 1986?… Hide your doctor's name and phone number?… Attach a note reminding yourself why you have someone's number?… Quickly enter contact info for an entire project team at a company?

Get Organized → Chapter 6 →

Calendar

Calendar keeps you one step ahead of yourself. Use it to plan your day, remember appointments, and prevent overscheduling. View your schedule by day, week, or month, or as an agenda that combines your tasks with your appointments. Attach notes to Calendar events and set alarms so you're reminded when they're about to happen.

In this chapter

▶ Enter appointment information in seconds

▶ Instantly schedule a year's worth of weekly meetings

▶ Mask secret events from prying eyes

Calendar tips

Enter simple events fast

Unless your days are always packed, you probably won't want to enter an end time and other details for events like a conference call or a TV show. Tap the line next to the start time in Day View, enter the name of the event, and you're done.

Events don't need times

Some events, such as the beginning and end of a fiscal quarter, don't have a start or end time. To schedule them, go to the day of the event and write a short description of the event. Calendar creates a new entry at the top of Day View. You can fill in the details later.

Create your own categories

Color-coded categories let you see at a glance how much time you're spending on work, play, and everything else. Calendar has four default categories: All, Business, Personal, and Unfiled. To color-code them as you like, see page 63.

The four Calendar views

Icons to look for

Calendar   Calendar

Calendar is a great application any way you look at it. In fact, you can look at it four different ways: Agenda, Day, Week, and Month. You'll probably use the first two views the most, but each view is useful.

Add background image to Agenda View

You can set Agenda View to be displayed against a light-blue background. It's a nice touch that quickly distinguishes Agenda View from other apps. In Agenda View, select **Options** > **Display Options** and check the **Background Image** box.

Quick agenda

Press the Calendar application button to see your day's agenda. Press it again to scroll through the four Calendar views. Go to **Options** > **Display Options** to make another view your default.

See the future

Calendar's great when you want to see what's happening today – or next year. In Month View, tap the **Year** button to make long-range plans for conferences and product launches.

Print your calendar
Use Palm® Desktop software to create a hard copy

1	Sync your handheld.
2	Open Palm Desktop software on your PC or Mac. Click **Calendar**. Click the **Print** icon.
3	Select print settings and print.

Four ways to check your calendar

Agenda View

Agenda View shows today's events and tomorrow's appointments. This view can also show your most urgent tasks or unread email messages (if an email program is installed). Tap any entry to see its contents.

Day View

Day View shows schedule highlights from a single day. The letters SMTWTFS appear at the top, with arrows pointing left and right. Tap the arrows to jump in one-week increments. To advance a single day, tap that day or press the navigator's right button. Note that this is the only view from which you can create new appointments.

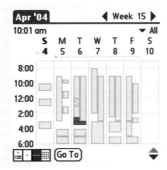

Week View

Scheduled events are marked by shaded bars – gray for Unfiled events, colors for other categories. Tap any bar to see details of the event. Week View is great for browsing your calendar to see when you'll be available.

Month View

Use Month View to check your long-term commitments and plans. Each day's events are marked by very small shaded boxes to indicate the amount of time scheduled for each category. Tap any day in the month to go straight to Day View.

Calendar menus

John is an investment banker in Los Angeles. He sets his Day View to start at 5 am and end at 4 pm by going to **Options** > **Preferences**. His twin brother, Omar, is a musician in Boston. His view starts at 11 am and ends at 11 pm.

Calendar is just as flexible as you are. Use it to keep up with your ever-changing schedule. Remind yourself of a call this afternoon, a barbecue next week, or a family reunion next year. Whether you work the day shift or the night shift – and even when you're feeling shiftless – you can change your Calendar settings to match your lifestyle.

No saving

You don't have to save new appointments. Just create them and they're saved automatically.

Like to plan ahead?

Unlike paper planners, the Calendar on your handheld reaches from January 1, 1904 (a Friday), to December 31, 2031 (a Wednesday).

Add contact info to an appointment

When you add an appointment to Calendar, you can quickly insert the phone number for the person you'll be meeting. Tap the line next to the hour of the appointment. From the menu bar, select **Options** > **Phone Lookup**. Select the name and tap **Add**. The person's name and telephone number are listed in the appointment entry.

Change the font

If you find yourself squinting to read event details, switch to a bigger, bolder font. Select **Font** from the **Options** menu. You have four styles to choose from.

Attach notes

Attach a note to a Calendar event with directions, things to bring, or other relevant info. In Day View, from the menu bar, select **Record** > **Attach Note**.

Menus in Agenda, Week, and Month Views

Options (Agenda, Week, or Month View)

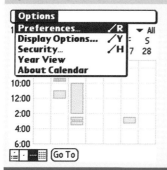

Use this menu to make all views match your scheduling needs. Use **Preferences** to change the settings for your reminder alarm. You might want an hour of warning to get ready for a big meeting, or just a few minutes to prepare for a lunch date. If you like to take the long view, in **Display Options**, select **Default View > Month**.

Menus in Day View

Record

Use the Record menu to add, delete, modify, and even share events. Tap an event, and then go to the menu and choose the command you want. Say you got word that the party this weekend is casual, not formal. Use **Attach Note** to remind yourself to leave the suit at home. Then use **Beam Event** to share the info with your date.

Edit

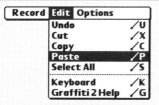

All the standard text input and correction tools are available. Don't ignore the Cut and Paste commands, especially when you're creating multiple meetings or events related to the same project or hobby.

Options

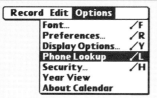

When you need to call a client to tell her you're running late for a business dinner, tap the event and use **Phone Lookup** to find her number fast.

Recurring events

Change the frequency
of a repeating event.
Remember to specify an
end date if you have one.

If your staff meeting is the first Wednesday of the month or your fencing team practices twice a week, no problem. The powerful repeat options in Calendar upstage paper planners by making sure you won't forget. Enter an appointment just once, no matter how many times it'll be repeated.

Set reminders

Recurring events can help you stick to some helpful routines.

▶ Set a weekly event reminder to update your Tasks lists or enter new contacts.

▶ Set a monthly reminder to clear your handheld of applications or info you no longer need.

▶ Set biannual events to catch up on taxes and review investments.

Use symbols to find events

Say you want to keep track of whose turn it is to buy lunch. Assign a unique symbol in the title field that's easy to write, such as an asterisk (✗²), and add it every time you pick up the check. Then use **Find** to see all those lunches in chronological order.

Save time with custom ShortCuts

Do you meet with the same person in the same place often, but not regularly enough to make it a recurring event? Make a ShortCut for the text you always write. For example: replace "Lunch with Bob at Jim's Coffee Shop" with the ShortCut **bob**. For more about ShortCuts, see page 42.

Create a recurring event

1 Make a new event or choose an existing event, and tap **Details**.

2 From the **Repeat** pick list, select one of the five standard repeat cycles.

3 Tap **OK**.

Schedule a recurring event

Daily or ongoing

Use this option to mark events that stretch over several days, such as conferences or long vacations. To create such an event, go to the Event Details screen, select **Repeat > Daily until**, and tap the end date.

Weekly

Keep track of weekly classes, favorite TV shows, or Sunday movie nights. Choose **Every week** or **Every other week** from the Event Details screen, or select **Other** for other intervals.

Monthly

Some events happen on the same date every month, while others might occur on the first Monday or third Thursday of each month. To schedule such an event from the Event Details screen, select **Repeat > Other** and tap the appropriate selections until the box displays the interval you want.

Yearly

Select **Yearly** to remember anniversaries or a tax deadline. (Contacts has an even better way to remember birthdays – see page 51.)

Real Life
Calendar

 Carmela's regular one-on-one meeting with her boss started out every other Tuesday, but her boss kept changing the day to fit his own schedule. It used to drive her crazy, and her day planner was a mess of crossed-out events. Now she uses the **Repeat > Other** function in the Event Details dialog box. When her boss changes the meeting to Friday morning, her Calendar automatically reschedules the event.

Alarms for untimed events

Some events, like your neighbor's open house or your nephew's graduation, may not yet have specific times. You can still set a reminder alarm for them. The reminder list displays the alarm message until you clear it. Alarms for untimed events go off at midnight.

Organize with Calendar

Share schedules

Say you have a new employee who has to attend a series of orientation seminars, or you have a vacation itinerary you want to share with your parents and housesitter. Create a Calendar category and beam the whole schedule to them.

Free for lunch?

To see whether you're free at a certain time or date, tap **Go To** in Day, Week, or Month View. Select the month, date, or day to quickly check your calendar or schedule a new event.

Go to

▶ To enter Calendar info with Palm Desktop software, see page 68.

▶ For more about categories, see page 24.

Add color to your calendar and watch your scheduling efficiency soar. Calendar's tools can help you get a handle on your most hectic weeks.

Start your week Sunday or Monday

To change the start of your week from Sunday to Monday, or vice versa, go to the Home screen and select **Preferences** > **Formats**.

Add names and numbers fast

Use **Phone Lookup** (/↑) when you're planning an event. It automatically takes you to Contacts, where you select a person's name and contact info and drop it into the event.

Purge events

1 Delete old events to save space. From Day View, select **Record** > **Purge**.

2 Select events older than a week, two weeks, three weeks, or a month.

3 Keep the box checked for **Save archive copy on PC** to back up all your events on your computer.

Calendar categories

Colors indicate event categories

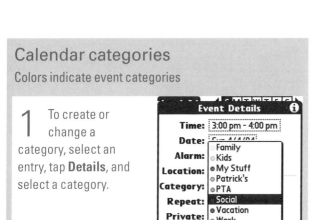

1 To create or change a category, select an entry, tap **Details**, and select a category.

2 To create a new category or edit an old one (such as "My Stuff"), select **Edit Categories**.

3 Tap **Edit** or **New** to name or rename a category and assign it one of the many colors. This makes it easy to scan Agenda, Day, Week, and Month Views.

Schedule downtime

Schedule free time as a recurring event and mark it as private. Go to **Options** > **Security** and select **Mask Records**. Your free time is now a block of lovely gray.

Mute alarms

To mute Calendar's alarms when you're at a meeting or luncheon, go to the Home screen and select **Prefs** > **Sounds & Alerts** > **Silent**. Turn the power off. Any alarms will be there for you when quiet time is over.

Calendar tips

▶ Create an event fast by tapping a time on the left side of Day View.

▶ When you don't have a specific start or end time, you can still create an event. Tap **No Time** when the Set Time box comes up. Events without times are marked by a diamond.

▶ When you schedule overlapping events, the bars in Week View appear side-by-side.

Hold on to important events

Repeating events don't get purged. So if you have a special event you want to remember, such as your graduation, set it up as an event that repeats every so many years.

Procrastinate

If you tap a task in Agenda View, the handheld goes directly to Tasks. From there, tap the Date column and delay the task for a day or a week. Just like that, it disappears from Agenda View.

Get Organized → Chapter 6 → Calendar →

More Calendar techniques

Real Life
Alarms & notes

 Charles is the secretary for a neighborhood group that meets on the first Tuesday of every month. He has an alarm reminder set for two days in advance of each meeting so that he remembers to use Tasks to set the agenda (by creating a category called "Meeting agenda" – see chapter 10). During the meeting, the agenda items show up on his Calendar's Agenda View. As each item is discussed, he checks it off.

Look ahead and back

Tap the top arrows

In Day, Week, and Month Views, the top-right part of the screen highlights the currently displayed period. Click the left and right arrows to quickly move back and forth through your calendar.

Jump around faster

In the same views, you can scan ahead or back without using the stylus. Just press right or left on the navigator to move forward or backward at day, week, or month intervals.

Keep an event under wraps

If anyone else uses your handheld, you might want to hide private events such as surprise parties. From the Home screen, go to **Options** > **Security** to show, mask, or hide entries. Mark an entry private to mask it with a gray bar or hide it completely. Remember that if you haven't set a password, masked and hidden entries are vulnerable.

☑ **Chapter 6: Did you discover how to...**

Enter appointment information in a few seconds?... Use categories to see how much time you'll be spending on that huge new work project?... Schedule a visit to the gym every three days?... Purge events but keep an archive, just in case?

Team your computer with your handheld

You get the most out of your handheld when you team it with Palm® Desktop software on your computer. Using Palm Desktop, you can quickly enter large amounts of information and then synchronize it all to your handheld. Even if you use another program to manage your Calendar and Contacts info, you still need Palm Desktop to sync.

In this chapter

▶ Rename your handheld

▶ Sync multiple handhelds to the same computer, or sync the same handheld to multiple computers

Sync often

Sync your handheld and your PC often. That way, you have a backup of your info at home when you're on the road with your handheld.

What is Palm Desktop software?

Palm Desktop is your handheld's indispensable companion on your computer. Even if you use Outlook, you need Palm Desktop because some applications, like Photos and Note Pad, are available only in Palm Desktop.

Want Outlook?

If you picked Palm Desktop when you went through installation, and now you want to switch to Outlook, reinsert the installation CD. From the Discover Your Handheld screen, select **Install Microsoft Outlook Conduits**.

Look for Quick Install on your desktop

Add applications to your handheld with Quick Install. Quick Install is automatically put on your desktop when you install Palm Desktop. (On a Mac, look for the Send To Handheld droplet in the palmOne folder. In OS X, drag it to the Dock to make it easier to drag stuff to transfer to your handheld.)

Palm Desktop software

Palm Desktop, which you operate from your PC, is a powerful way to create and manage your handheld's info.

Palm Desktop lives on your computer, not your handheld. If you elected to use Outlook or the Mac iSync application to manage your synchronizing, chances are you don't see Palm Desktop that much. But it handles the HotSync® process and a whole lot more. Perhaps most importantly, Palm Desktop is the means by which you get applications from the Internet to your handheld.

Palm Desktop menu highlights: Windows

Tools > Options

Customize settings for Palm Desktop. Calendar is the default screen when you open Palm Desktop. Change it here. Then select among the tabs to set security, activate or disable alarms, choose among a variety of color themes, and auto-save information.

Tools > Addins > Delete Duplicates

Find and remove duplicate entries in Calendar, Tasks, Contacts, and Memos by using Delete Duplicates. It identifies entries that are partial matches, which often happens when you beam a lot and receive files and entries from other handhelds.

HotSync > Custom

Fine-tune your HotSync settings so your handheld and your PC exchange info exactly the way you want. Conduits are the settings that determine what happens when you sync. Each app has its own conduit. For more about conduits, see page 72.

Printing

Print layouts

Sometimes it's great to have a hard copy to tack up on your wall. With Palm Desktop, you can print your calendars, tasks, and even address lists by category. On a Mac, you can even choose the layout you want. Select **File** > **Print** and choose the layout you want, edit a layout, or add a new layout that fits your style.

Printing for a binder (Mac)

To make binder-ready printouts, select **File** > **Print** > **Edit Layout** > **Holes**. The number of holes you can make corresponds to the layout size you choose. Click **Cut Lines** for a dashed line showing where to hole-punch.

Help

The online Palm Desktop Help system is on the Help menu. Select the **Contents**, **Index**, or **Find** tab to get no-nonsense help quick.

If you use a Mac

You can find out more about Mac Palm Desktop by going to your palmOne folder and reading the PDF file in the Documentation folder.

Palm Desktop menu highlights: Mac

File > Merge

If you and a colleague want to have a copy of each other's calendar, contacts, and business memos, you can use Merge to combine your info. Remember, however, that merging is a complete, two-way swap of all your info. It might be easier to copy or beam selected entries.

HotSync > Install Handheld Files

This command opens a dialog box where you drag files to install them during your next synchronization. Note that in the Destination field, you can make the application install to an expansion card.

Preferences > Alarms

If you always add alarms to appointments, you can set a preference that automatically adds an alarm to every appointment you create, using the options you select. You can also have alarms appear on your Mac as well as on your handheld.

Enter info from your computer

Icons to look for on your computer

Palm Desktop   Palm Desktop

Both Windows (left) and Mac (right) display desktop icons for easy access to Palm Desktop from your computer.

Date & Time Stamp (Windows)

Paste the date or time into any text field by pressing **CTRL+SHIFT+T** or **CTRL+SHIFT+D**. Press **CTRL+SHIFT+T+D** to paste both the time and the date.

Create duplicate entries faster (Mac)

If you're entering multiple entries that have information in common, duplicate an existing entry and then make changes to it. Highlight the existing entry and select **Edit** > **Duplicate Contact**.

Your handheld and your PC make an especially good team when you've got a lot of info to enter. Whether or not your little black book is already in electronic form, creating entries in Palm Desktop can be faster than writing or tapping on your handheld. Special features in Palm Desktop make input even quicker. All of the techniques on these pages apply to your computer, not your handheld.

Enter info quickly

It's easy to enter info in Palm Desktop. On the left side of Palm Desktop, click the application. Next, click **New** in the lower-left corner. To edit info, click **Edit** in the lower-left corner. A quick way to change current entries or add new ones is to double-click an entry or a blank space in any application.

Find an archived address

1 If you've archived or deleted a Contacts entry by mistake, open Palm Desktop and click **Contacts**. Select **File > Open Archive** (Mac: **File > Open**).

2 Click the archive file you want and search for the entry. Export it (**File > Export**) and close the archive. Then import it (**File > Import**) into Contacts.

Use templates for speed (Mac)

In Calendar, Contacts, Memos, and Tasks, you can create templates for frequently repeated items, like people from the same company. Make a new entry or open an existing entry, and then select **Create > New Template**. Give it a name and it appears on the Create menu of your PC. To create a new entry from the template, just select it from the Create menu.

Send info to other apps (Windows)

To easily transfer information in Palm Desktop to other applications, select **Edit > Send To**, and then pick **MS Word** or **MS Excel**. Send your task lists and memos to Word or your Expense items to Excel and then edit, email, or print.

Multiple users, multiple computers

Two PCs, one handheld

If you have two computers, insert the installation CD and install Palm Desktop on both. When you sync to the first one, you create a username. When you sync to the second computer, it will recognize the username you already created. When you make changes on one computer, your handheld can sync it to the other.

Multiple handhelds, one computer

Anyone with a palmOne™ handheld older than yours can sync to your version of Palm Desktop. If your computer doesn't recognize the handheld, you get the alert box, "Do you want to create a new account for this user?" Click **Yes**, and Palm Desktop automatically recognizes that handheld whenever you sync.

If you have a computer at work and another one at home, your handheld can link them together. A few tips can make it easier to keep everything straight.

Where's my info?

If you share Palm Desktop with another person, your handheld still syncs automatically with your username. If you can't find the information you just entered, check to see if you mistakenly put it under the wrong username.

Personalize it

One user per handheld

Your handheld can have only one "user" – if you share it, you also share its files, entries, and applications. But you can password-protect sensitive info. See page 34.

Rename your handheld: Windows

1 From the **Tools** menu, select **Users**. Highlight your username and click **Rename**.

2 Enter the new username and click **OK**.

3 Sync. Your new username appears in the upper-right corner of your handheld's HotSync screen.

Username vs. Owner name

HotSync PatrickAmes
HotSync operation complete.

Local Modem

▼ Cradle/Cable

Log Help

Your username is what HotSync Manager uses to keep your handheld's info straight when it syncs with your PC. It appears on your handheld in the upper-right corner of the HotSync screen. This name is different than your Owner name, which you can find by selecting **Home** > **Prefs** > **Owner**. The Owner name simply identifies your handheld as yours.

Personalize it (Macs only)

Palm Desktop has dozens of different color themes to keep your schedule looking unique enough from your spouse's. Select **Preferences** > **Decor** and pick a color theme you can instantly recognize.

Use different usernames

If you use another handheld or share a computer with someone who does, make sure each handheld has a different username.

Rename your handheld: Mac

1 Open **HotSync**, click the **Users** sub-menu, and choose **Edit Users**.

2 Highlight your username, click **Edit**, and change the name.

3 The new username appears on the HotSync screen of your handheld the next time you sync.

New computer, same handheld

First, sync your handheld with your old computer so the info on your handheld is up-to-date. After you set up your new computer, insert the installation CD and follow the instructions to connect your handheld. The installation program detects your handheld's username and syncs your info to the new computer. You may have to reinstall the desktop component of some of the apps you added from the CD, such as RealOne® Player.

Share calendars

If you share a computer and want to see what your partner has going on, simply select the other username in Palm Desktop. For instructions on protecting info, see page 34.

Add favorites to a menu (Mac)

If you have an entry or file you open often, open it and select **Locate** > **Add to Menu**. The entry is immediately added to the Locate menu list. Tap **Delete** to remove it from the Locate menu.

Customize synchronization

When you sync, info on your handheld and Palm Desktop is automatically exchanged and updated. Conduits control how the info is shared.

The relationship between your handheld and computer is characterized by one of four settings:

▶ Synchronize the files
▶ Desktop overrides handheld
▶ Handheld overrides Desktop
▶ Do nothing

In general, don't mess with conduits

Be careful with your conduits. The default settings make sure the most current info syncs between your handheld and computer.

When to mess with conduits

Change your conduits when there's an app you don't want to sync, or you want the info on your handheld to overwrite the info on your computer, or vice versa.

Import contacts from other apps

You can import info into Palm Desktop from most contact programs and from other applications such as Microsoft Excel. For details, see your Tungsten E Handbook, available from the Help menu of Palm Desktop or as a free download from www.palmOne.com/support/tungstene.

What are conduits?

▶ Conduits are settings that manage how your handheld's applications sync with your computer.

▶ You set conduits in Palm Desktop, not on your handheld. Select **HotSync > Custom** (on a Mac, select **HotSync > Conduit Settings**).

▶ Different users can have different conduit settings. The username shown in the Custom dialog box in Palm Desktop is the one being changed.

▶ Conduits for palmOne™ VersaMail™, Documents To Go, and other applications have custom settings.

Changing conduits

1 From the **HotSync** menu, select **Custom** (or **Conduit Settings** on a Mac).

2 Select any conduit from the list and click **Change** (or **Settings** on a Mac).

3 Choose what you want the conduit to do. This affects only your next sync. To make the change permanent, select **Set as Default**.

What can I do with conduits?

▶ Make photos sync with your home PC, but not with your work PC.

▶ Set your email so that it won't sync, saving time.

▶ Have your PC overwrite your handheld if your spouse accidentally beams you the wrong task list.

Changing from Outlook (Windows only)

If you've set up your PC to sync with Palm Desktop, you can change to Outlook anytime. Insert your installation CD and select **Install Microsoft Outlook Conduits**.

Back up Palm Desktop (Mac)

If you like to keep your info extra safe, save a copy of your Palm Desktop data as a backup. Select **File** > **Save a Copy** and give the backup file a name and location. This saves a snapshot of the info at the moment you saved the copy.

Change your view (Mac)

Choose any list view from the View menu. Arrange it to your liking and choose **Memorize View** from the pick list in the upper-left corner. The new arrangement is now listed in the View pick list.

More Palm Desktop time-savers

Some of the coolest features of Palm Desktop defy easy categorization. Here are a few more time-savers to try out on your computer.

To make the password on your handheld protect info in Palm Desktop, select **Tools** > **Options** > **Security** and check the box.

Choose your alarms (Windows)

Arm your computer with alarm sounds, too. Select **Tools** > **Options** > **Alarms**.

Online help

Go to **Help** > **Online Support** to directly access palmOne's worldwide support.

Save time with Palm Desktop

Drag and drop events

Need to reschedule an appointment? In the Day View of Palm Desktop's Calendar, drag an event to any date in the months shown to the right.

Reschedule events

When someone reschedules a lunch, a meeting, or any other event, edit the old entry rather than creating a new one from scratch.

Cycle through views (Mac)

To cycle through the Calendar views, click the **Date Book** icon in the tool bar. Quickly scan your events in Agenda, Day, and Week Views.

☑ **Chapter 7: Did you discover how to...**

Adjust conduits to sync Calendar but not Contacts?... Dig up a phone number you thought you'd never need again?... Enter an officeful of contacts fast?... Share your handheld with someone else without going crazy (or letting them in on your secrets)?

Get Connected → Chapter 8 →

Get in sync

Team up your handheld and your computer to get the most out of both. Synchronizing your handheld and your computer automatically creates a backup of all your important info and lets you transfer new info, applications, photos, music, and files from your computer to your handheld or an expansion card.

What you can do by synchronizing

▶ Transfer games to your handheld after you've downloaded them from the web.

▶ Transfer new songs to your expansion card to listen to on the morning commute.

▶ Keep a work calendar that's always up-to-date.

▶ Back up your handheld info as often as necessary (at least once a week, but preferably every day).

In this chapter

▶ How to sync
▶ Install applications on your handheld
▶ Advanced ways to sync

How it works

When you sync information, it isn't just poured from one device into the other. Info that's new or changed in your desktop software is added and changed on your handheld, and vice versa. Info that hasn't changed stays put.

When was your last sync?

To find out the last time you synchronized, from the Home screen, tap the **HotSync®** icon and then tap **Log**.

Sync your handheld

When your handheld is on and connected to your computer, tap the icon where the red circle is to start synchronization.

If you tap the Star icon and nothing happens, go to the Home screen and tap the HotSync icon there. When the screen (below) appears, tap the large icon in the middle of the screen to begin synchronization.

Synchronizing is simple. Use the USB HotSync cable that came with your handheld to make sure info on your handheld is saved to your computer.

How to sync

First, install Palm® Desktop software

You can't sync without Palm Desktop, which is included on the installation CD.

Connect the HotSync cable

Plug one end of the cable into a USB port on your PC. Plug the other end into your handheld.

Tap the HotSync icon

Turn your handheld on. Tap the Star icon in the upper-right corner of the writing area. Synchronization starts. How can you tell? Among other things, if your system sounds are turned on, you'll hear the HotSync chime.

Look for the moving arrows

Arrows in the HotSync Progress box on your PC move, letting you know the sync is in process.

Check the info

When the sync is complete, the info on your handheld should be the same as the info on your computer.

Synchronizing tips

Sync regularly

Get in the habit of performing a sync at a certain time every day, and you won't have to worry about the last time you did. When you sync regularly, you create a reliable backup and keep your info up-to-date on both your computer and your handheld.

Canceling a sync

If you decide to cancel a sync in progress, be patient. Stopping the synchronizing process can take a minute or two.

Faster after the first sync

After you sync for the first time, the process becomes much faster, since your handheld and PC exchange only info that has changed since the last sync.

USB is simple and fast

The easiest way to sync is to use the USB cable that came with your handheld.

HotSync

Connecting with the desktop using Cradle/Cable

[Cancel]

Your handheld's screen during synchronization.

Why sync?

The process not only keeps your info current, it also guarantees that if you ever misplace or lose your handheld, all your info will still exist on your PC.

How to tell whether you've done a sync

From the Home screen, tap the **HotSync** icon and tap **Log** at the bottom of the screen. If you've never synchronized, it will say so there.

Icon to look for

HotSync

Advanced sync techniques

For advanced techniques and ways to customize the sync process, see page 84.

The sync sound

A three-note chime signals the start and end of the synchronizing process.

Get Connected → Chapter 8 → Get in sync →

Sync settings

Sharing a PC

If multiple people share a PC but have their own handhelds, each owner must create a unique username so that Palm Desktop can keep their info separate.

Once you're comfortable with the HotSync process, you'll understand how powerful synchronizing can be. It not only backs up your handheld but also transfers any changes you make on your PC to your handheld, or vice versa. HotSync is also your link to stuff you've downloaded onto your handheld, including software, photos, and MP3s.

Find your username: Windows and Mac
Look for your username in the upper-right corner of the screen

During your first sync, you assign a username to your handheld. The same name is associated with your info in Palm Desktop. Several handhelds can sync with the same computer. Find your username on your handheld by going to **Home** > **HotSync**. The name appears in the upper-right corner.

Sync better with management tools

Conduits

A conduit is a small program that specifies how (and whether) info is exchanged between your computer and your handheld. Each application has its own conduit. To learn more about conduits, see page 72.

HotSync Manager

HotSync Manager monitors the port your computer uses for synchronizing, launching the appropriate conduits. In Windows, HotSync Manager is part of Palm Desktop software; on Macs, it's a stand-alone application.

Conduit defaults

Leave the conduits on their default settings unless you need to overwrite data or you want to save time by avoiding the sync process for an application you haven't used in a long time. To make a change apply to future syncs, in Windows, check the **Set as default** box. On a Mac, select the **Make Default** button.

Usernames

Your username ensures that Palm Desktop can distinguish your information from somebody else's. To change your username, see page 70.

Sync with Windows and Mac

Your handheld is designed to sync easily with Windows-based PCs and Macs running OS 9.1 or higher or Mac OS X 10.1.2 to 10.2.6. Both platforms use programs called conduits to transfer info from computer to handheld and back again. Both also use Palm Desktop, which syncs seamlessly with your handheld. To learn about conduits and Palm Desktop, see page 72.

Windows tips

▶ To sync with Outlook, reinsert the installation CD and click **Install Microsoft Outlook Conduits**.

▶ You can customize the synchronization between Outlook and your handheld by using Palm Desktop software. Click any Outlook conduit and click **Change**.

Mac tips

▶ To use OS X's calendar and address books instead of Palm Desktop software, download and install the iSync Palm Conduit from www.apple.com.

▶ Because Palm Desktop has different features than your handheld, the ways in which information is transferred during a sync are not always obvious. For details, see Palm Desktop's Help topic about transferring info to your handheld.

Trouble with the HotSync process?

If you're having trouble synchronizing, see page 82.

Add software

Expansion cards

Expansion cards (sold separately) give you more memory to store all kinds of applications and files. For details, see page 138.

Find great software

Check palmOne.com for thousands of cool apps. For more about software, see chapter 14.

Add applications so you can do more with your handheld. Pick apps you'll use to keep track of business travel, manage your nutrition, or find a great restaurant. Many apps come in a free trial version. Download them from the web and sync them to your handheld. There's no better way to explore what your handheld can do than to check out some of the 20,000 apps available.

Install applications: Windows

Double-click the **palmOne™ Quick Install** icon on the desktop. Drag application files into the appropriate window (for either your handheld or an expansion card) or click the **Add** button and browse for the files. Compressed files you drag to the open Quick Install window are automatically decompressed. Sync to

Uninstalled files

If a file you meant to install remains on the Quick Install list, your handheld or card might be full, or the file might be incompatible. On a Mac, a file that remains in the Install Handheld Files dialog box indicates a similar problem. Compatible files end with .prc, .pdb, or .scr.

Get classic games

Get games designed specifically for your handheld. Classic arcade games like Asteroids and Centipede can be found on the Atari Retro and Sega Classics expansion cards; see page 161.

Download free or cheap apps

Many sites on the web have apps you can download for free or for a nominal cost. Be careful that the app is compatible with Palm OS 5.2. Investigate reviews and ratings to see how well the app works.

Share apps with friends

Many apps, especially freeware and trial versions, can be beamed to other handhelds. From your Home screen, select **App** > **Beam**. Be sure it's compatible with your friend's handheld.

Your version number

Tungsten E handhelds use version 5.2 of the Palm OS®.

Find new apps

Newly installed applications show up on the **Home** screen in the **All** and **Unfiled** categories.

Go to

▶ For more about expansion cards, see pages 16 and 138.

▶ To shop for software, see page 132.

▶ If a new app freezes your handheld, see page 20.

Install applications: Mac

On a Mac, open **Palm Desktop**. From the HotSync menu, select **Install Handheld Files**. Drag the application files to this window or click the **Add To List** button and browse for the files. Sync to transfer files.

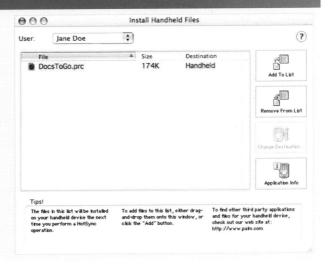

Out of sync

HotSync Log

Last HotSync operation:
3/9/04, 7:30 am

OK Install
OK iSync Conduit
OK Photos
OK Note Pad
OK Documents To Go
OK Adobe Reader
OK Install
OK Backup

(Done)

The HotSync Log shows what happened during synchronizing.

Your handheld is designed to work with your computer seamlessly. But there may be times when you need to reinstall info or apps, particularly if you let the battery run out completely or if you've had to perform a hard reset for any reason. There may be times, too, when the HotSync process doesn't seem to be working. Learn how to fix it with these techniques.

Extra-safe backups

Back up info on a separate expansion card. If you have a Mac, you can make a backup of your info on your computer – a backup of a backup, in effect. In Mac Palm Desktop, select **File > Save a Copy**.

Go to

▶ For info about the battery, see page 18.

▶ To reset your handheld, see page 20.

Restore all info from Windows

1	Click the **HotSync** icon in the Windows system tray.
2	From the HotSync Manager menu, select **Custom** and choose a username.
3	Select an application from the conduit list and click **Change**.
4	Select **Desktop overwrites handheld** and click **OK**.
5	Repeat until all conduit settings are changed; then click **Done** to activate, and sync.

Troubleshooting checklist
If synchronizing doesn't work...

Check the cable and other connections	Is the cable plugged into the right port? Is the USB plug working?
Check your handheld's HotSync Log for alert messages	In HotSync Manager, select the **HotSync** menu and click **View Log**.
Quit and restart HotSync Manager	In Windows, quit and reopen HotSync Manager. On a Mac, disable local HotSync, wait a few seconds, and then re-enable.

More troubleshooting options

▶ Quit HotSync Manager and restart your computer.

▶ Turn off startup programs and system extensions. They might be interfering with your ports.

▶ Quit any communication programs that are running, such as Internet software.

▶ If you're trying to sync to an expansion card and having trouble, check to see if it's full (select **Home** > **Card Info**) and make sure it's unlocked.

▶ If all else fails, go to www.palmOne.com/ support/tungstene. See page xii.

Restore all info from a Mac

1 Double-click **HotSync Manager** in the Palm folder.

2 From the **HotSync** menu, select conduit settings and choose a username.

3 Select an application from the list and click **Conduit settings**.

4 Select **Macintosh overwrites handheld** and click **OK**.

5 Repeat until all conduit settings are changed; close the Conduit Settings window, and sync.

Get Connected → Chapter 8 → Get in sync →

More synchronization techniques

Learn more

For details about advanced synchronization options, see the Tungsten E Handbook at Palm Desktop's Help menu or visit www.palmOne.com/support. See page xii.

Sync to multiple computers

You can sync your handheld to more than one computer. See page 70.

Add it with Addit (Windows)

Freely available at www.palmOne.com, Addit helps you pick the best apps to add to your handheld, and even manages downloading, payment, and installation.

The USB cable is the most common way to sync, but it's not the only way.

Advanced synchronization options	
Connection	Comments
Infrared ("Beaming" sync)	
Wireless, but slower and uses more battery power than USB.	You must activate your computer's IR port (if it has one).
Bluetooth® technology	
Like an infrared sync, but can be performed over a longer distance.	Convenient, but requires a Bluetooth adapter for the Tungsten E.
Modem	
Syncs between two modems.	Requires more setup.
LAN	
Syncs with corporate data via modem or Internet. For Windows only.	Should be done with the aid of your network administrator.

☑ **Chapter 8: Did you discover how to...**

Make your handheld's Calendar reflect the meeting invitations you created last night in Outlook?... Find a fitness training app online, and install it?... Immediately undermine that app by installing an addictive game?... Figure out why a sync isn't working?

Beaming

Beaming puts you in direct touch with a community of handheld users. Use it to share the wealth. Just about everything on your handheld can be beamed, from your Tasks agenda to your Note Pad doodles. Keep colleagues up-to-date on your schedule and share photos with friends. Get them to share their stuff, too – beaming is a two-way street, as long as you're beaming to another Palm OS® handheld.

In this chapter

► Beam your business card

► Beam whole applications

► Beam an entire category of contact entries

Beaming facts

► Your handheld can beam across the width of a typical kitchen table.

► If your mobile phone is infrared-enabled, you can beam names and numbers to it.

► Your handheld uses slightly more power when its ability to receive beamed info is turned on.

Attach notes to received items

Right after someone beams you a business card or other information, attach a note to the new entry. Write down what you talked about so you can refer to it later. For instructions, see page 44.

Memory requirements

The handheld you beam to must have at least twice as much free memory as the item you beam. Space is almost never a problem for small items like business cards and simple notes, but it can be an issue when you're beaming or receiving an entire category or application.

Beaming basics

Beam your calendar

Beam your boss your business appointments for the week. From Day View of Calendar, select **Menu** > **Record** > **Beam Category**. Make sure you have a category for business appointments.

▶ To learn about categories, see page 24.

▶ To learn how to get organized with Calendar, see page 62.

Choose the right info

Make sure you've selected the right entry before you beam it. The process is usually so fast that it's hard to stop in progress.

Beam securely

Whenever you beam something private, make sure you're beaming it to the right person's handheld.

Whether you're sending a quick request for info to a colleague or a whole category of stuff to friends, the beaming process is the same. But the possibilities are endless. Beam home repair tasks to your family, beam your hairdresser's name and number to a friend, beam your gumbo recipe (with photo, but without secret ingredient) to your chief culinary rival.

How to beam

1 Make sure both devices are turned on and pointed at each other.

2 Select the entry or category to beam, open the **Record** menu, and select **Beam**.

3 A dialog box opens on the recipient's handheld, asking whether to accept the information.

4 Before accepting beamed info, assign it to a category; otherwise, it goes to Unfiled.

5 If the recipient agrees to receive the info, both people see details about the info.

How beaming works

What is IR?

Infrared technology (IR) is found in most handhelds, mobile phones, and laptop computers. You can't see IR, it can't hurt you, and it works only over short distances.

Distance

Your handheld's IR works between any two IR devices within a meter (about 39 inches) of each other. The IR port on your handheld is on the top of the device, and can share info only with devices within a direct line of sight.

Beam faster

To maximize beaming speed, set the devices on a flat surface about a foot apart (but not directly touching), and avoid areas with flickering or neon lights. Temperature extremes can also affect beaming.

Beaming in action

▶ At a study group, each person brings notes from a different chapter and beams them to the group.

▶ Traveling salespeople beam the previous day's sales logs to colleagues.

▶ A maid of honor beams the updated schedule to the whole wedding party.

What you can beam

▶ Any entry currently displayed in Calendar, Contacts, Tasks, Notes, or Memos

▶ The contents of any category available in Contacts, Tasks, or Memos

▶ Your business card or another designated entry in Contacts

▶ Applications installed in memory that are not locked

▶ Individual files such as photos, application documents, and more

Beaming applications

▶ To identify beamable applications, select **Home** > **Menu** > **App** > **Beam**. Anything without a lock icon can be beamed. To learn how to lock and unlock individual entries, see page 35.

▶ Applications built into your handheld, such as Calendar or Contacts, as well as some third-party apps, can't be beamed.

Share info fast

Real Life
Beam calendars

 Marla and John are married airline pilots. Every week was a scheduling nightmare until they both got handhelds. Now they beam their schedules to each other at the beginning of every month. They each maintain a category with their own schedules. When either of them views All in Calendar, both of their schedules appear together.

Beam and receive whole categories from Calendar, Contacts, Tasks, Memos, and other applications to quickly share lots of info. Whether you want to share a bunch of photos or a combination of contacts and deadlines, there's no easier way to pass along stuff to the people who need it (or just can't wait to see it).

Beaming on/off

When you turn off your handheld's ability to receive beamed info (**Prefs** > **Power**), it doesn't affect your ability to beam info.

Beam a category

Beaming a category works just like beaming a single item, except that you select **Beam Category** from the menu. You must be viewing the category as a whole – you can't beam a category when an individual entry is displayed. If you're receiving a category of info and don't have a preset category, create a category before the beam and select it when you receive the beamed info.

Beam applications

Beaming entire applications can be easier than installing them from scratch, but you can't beam copy-protected apps. Files created or used by a program must be beamed separately. Select **Home** > **Menu** > **App** > **Beam** to beam anything that isn't a single entry or a category.

Beam photos

1 Open Photos from the Home screen. (If you don't see it, install it from your installation CD.)

2 From either the thumbnail view or the list view, select the photo you want to beam. Use the navigator, since tapping a photo will open it. Select **Menu** > **Photos** > **Beam Photo**.

3 Position your handheld close to the receiving handheld and beam it.

Swap numbers

If you think a friend should meet one of your contacts (or vice versa), beam the info. For more about Contacts, see page 49.

Beam tasks

You can beam a task or an entire category of tasks. Nothing feels better than creating tasks for someone else and then beaming them all their assignments at once.

Beam from an expansion card

To beam info or applications from an expansion card, select **Beam** from the Home screen's **App** menu. Tap **Beam From** at the top of the screen and select the expansion card.

Quickly beam your business card

First, designate an entry as your business card (see page 50). Beam your business card by holding down the **Contacts** button until the beaming message ("Searching…") appears.

Beam a game

Many apps and games can be beamed. Just go to the Home screen and select **Menu** > **App** > **Beam**, select the game, and tap **Beam**. Some commercial games, like Handmark Scrabble, let you beam a trial version of the game that can be played several times.

Go to

▶ To learn more about Photos, see chapter 13.

Troubleshooting and more

Beam to a phone

You can beam single contacts from your handheld to an IR-equipped mobile phone. Be sure the phone's IR is turned on. Put the two devices close together, beam the entry from Contacts, and follow your phone's instructions for saving beamed info.

Beam to your TV

Some apps take creative advantage of beaming, including some very cool shareware and freeware. One program even turns your handheld into the ultimate universal remote control. For more about finding software online, see page 132.

When beaming doesn't work, the problem is usually easy to fix. Answer the questions below to identify some of the most common beaming problems. If you still have trouble beaming or receiving beams, visit www.palmOne.com/support for help.

Troubleshooting checklist

▶ Do both devices have IR capability?

▶ Do both devices have beaming turned on? From the Home screen, select **Prefs** > **Power** > **Beam Receive** > **On**.

▶ Are the devices on a flat surface, pointed toward each other, no more than a meter apart but not touching?

▶ Does the receiving device have enough memory to accommodate the beamed item?

▶ Is another wireless device in use nearby, such as a wireless keyboard? If so, it may be interfering.

▶ Are you beaming to a handheld with an older Palm OS? If so, some of the info you beamed may not be received.

▶ Do any currently running apps disable beaming?

☑ **Chapter 9: Did you discover how to...**

Get your partners' project schedules onto your handheld?... Beam a new recruit the phone numbers of your alumni group/darts team/fan club?... Beam your business card with one hand, on an elevator?... Share an addictive game with loved ones?

Tasks

Say goodbye to that familiar "I know I'm forgetting something" feeling. The Tasks application helps you track, organize, and prioritize your responsibilities. Use it to keep your important goals and responsibilities from getting lost in a pile of less urgent stuff. Tasks can provide a huge return on a small investment in time. Take a few minutes to plot all your to-do items, and you'll find yourself getting a lot more done.

In this chapter

▶ Organize tasks
▶ Create the ultimate to-do list
▶ View things you need to do this week
▶ Use Tasks as a study aid
▶ Set alarms with tasks

Fast tasks

To create a new task fast, open Tasks and begin writing in the Graffiti® 2 writing area. A new task is created automatically.

First things first

Use priorities to make urgent tasks stand out. Tasks can be prioritized from 1 (highest priority) to 5 (lowest). Regularly update priorities to reflect your shifting daily and weekly schedule.

Tasks show up in Calendar

When you create tasks, they automatically show up in Calendar's Agenda View – just tap a task to see it. When a task is past due, it appears on your agenda with an exclamation point.

Duplicate tasks to save time

Create a task that shares the due date and category of another by highlighting an existing task, tapping **New**, and changing what the task is.

Tasks menus

Icon to look for

Tasks

Hide completed tasks

Few things are more
satisfying than crossing
a nagging responsibility
off your list. Make your
to-do items disappear
once they're checked off.
From the menu bar, select
Options > Preferences
and uncheck the **Show
Completed Tasks** box. This
doesn't delete the tasks; it
only hides them from view.

Use categories

Tasks you don't finish on
a given day get rolled over
to the next day. To avoid
long lists of overdue tasks,
create long- and short-
term categories, such as
"This Week" and "This
Month," all with no due
date. Check these holding
bins and reassign tasks
to other categories when
you have due dates.

Use Tasks to stay on top of all the
things you need to get done. View
your tasks as a complete list, by due
date, or by category. Review your
tasks every day to save yourself time
and energy.

Calendar similarities

Tasks and Calendar share many of the same menu
commands. If you've mastered Calendar, you should
have no trouble with Tasks. To learn more about
Calendar, see chapter 6.

In Calendar's Agenda
View, tasks are displayed
underneath events, so
you can see what's past
due and what's coming
up. Check the box when
you complete a task, or
tap the task to go directly
to Tasks.

Tasks menus

Record

Select **Purge** to delete all the tasks that are marked as completed. Check the **Save archive copy on PC** box if you want to keep a backup. To beam an individual task, tap **Beam Task**. To beam a whole category of to-dos to a coworker, friend, or family member, tap **Beam Category**.

Note: Send commands show up on menus only after you have installed the SMS or VersaMail app from the installation CD.

Options

When you're making a task list for calls you need to return, Phone Lookup comes in handy. Tap **New** to create a task. Select **Options** > **Phone Lookup**, tap the contact you need to call, and tap **Add** to instantly add the number to the task. The Options menu also lets you change the font and set preferences and security settings.

Options > Preferences

In **Preferences**, check the **Show Completed Tasks** box to see the tasks you've completed. Check the **Record Completion Date** box to change an item's due date. You can also set the alarm sound for Tasks and show or hide due dates, priorities, and categories.

Back up your tasks

Tasks are archived on your PC when you synchronize, giving you a useful log of your activities.

Let it go

If you'd rather forget what you've done, uncheck the **Save archive copy on PC** box when you delete or purge tasks.

Sort order

In **Preferences**, you have four choices for sorting tasks. The most important ones deal with due dates and priority.

Mastering Tasks

Use due dates, priority settings, and categories to accomplish more. Alarms and recurring tasks make it even easier to know when things are due. By adding new tasks to your to-do list as soon as they come up, you'll have the ultimate to-do list nearby at all times.

Tasks until 2031

Your handheld's calendar reaches to 2031 – create due dates for tasks from now until then.

Schedule repeating tasks

Schedule repeating tasks to remember when to put out the trash, call for a dentist appointment, or pick up the kids. Select a task, tap **Details**, and tap the **Repeat** pick list. Repeat tasks daily until a specified date, or create customized deadlines. After you schedule a repeating or continuous task, the Repeat icon appears next to the task in the Tasks list.

Meet your goals

Create a category called "Goals" and create one task per month with something you want to do. Attach a note with details or reminders of why it's important.

Don't overdo dates

Be realistic when you set due dates in Tasks. Planning more items than you can reasonably expect yourself to complete won't boost your productivity.

Personalizing Tasks

Use dates

If you're deadline-driven, be sure to check the **Show Due Dates** option in **Preferences**. Use the **Date** view to see what's due today, what's due next week, and what's past due. Check and update your due dates daily. Tracking by date shows the selected task in the Agenda View of Calendar.

Set priorities

If you tend to become overwhelmed by a long list of competing responsibilities and goals, use priority ratings to decide where to turn your attention first. You can give tasks a priority rating from 1 (most urgent) to 5 (least urgent).

Define categories

Creating custom categories can help you efficiently sort through your tasks. Think about the different areas of your life and create categories that match those areas. The categories might be subdivided, such as "Work calls" and "Work meetings," or more general, such as "Work." To learn more about categories, see page 24.

Set an alarm for a task

1 Select a task that has a due date and tap **Details.**

2 Tap the **Alarm** box. The Set Alarm dialog box appears.

3 Select the time you want the alarm to go off and the number of days (if any) before the due date.

Beaming tasks

Share your tasks with coworkers, family, and friends who have an infrared-capable handheld. Open the **Record** menu and select **Beam Item.**

What you can do with Tasks

▶ Keep separate work, home, and weekend task categories

▶ Assign tasks for next week or next month, without specific due dates

▶ Set a task alarm to chime from one to five days before the task is due

▶ Assign a different alarm sound for a task. Select **Menu > Options > Preferences > Alarm Sound** and pick an appropriate sound. If you use Tasks to remind yourself to make phone calls, select the Phone sound.

Categorize tasks

Create the same categories in Tasks that you create in Contacts and Calendar. This gives you a coherent structure for organizing your days.

More Tasks techniques

The Tasks application works best when you use it every day. Spend five minutes a day updating your tasks, and you'll save hours every week.

Two ideas for Tasks

Print your lists

Use Palm® Desktop software to print out your to-do list, and tape it to a wall for handy reference.

Plan a vacation

Got a big vacation coming up? Create a Tasks category for the trip. Set high priorities for the things that need to be done first like buying tickets, getting visas, and making reservations. Set lower priorities for packing.

Create "task cards" as study aides

By creating a task as a question and attaching a note with the answer, you can create handy flash cards. For example, a student of French might enter "house" as a task, and "la maison" as the note. Enter the information in Palm Desktop software, synchronize, and practice when you're on the go.

Meet big deadlines

Create categories for specific deliverables, such as "Sales presentation" or "School board report." Keep yourself on task by creating easily achievable tasks for each step toward completion, such as "confirm time for presentation." Track deadlines and priorities through the Agenda View in Calendar.

☑ Chapter 10: Did you discover how to...

Distinguish important tasks from trivial ones?... Get rid of all the stuff you've done but keep a backup copy, just in case?... Set a recurring task to move your car on street-cleaning day?... Use Tasks to get ready for your big exam?

Memos

Memos let you record essential but easy-to-forget information. Write complete sentences and paragraphs, or just jot down your musings and lists. Keep track of movies you intend to rent or CDs you want to buy. Recipes, meeting notes, directions, quotations, and personal goals all make great memos, too.

In this chapter
▶ Organize memos
▶ Move through memos
▶ Create categories

Go to
▶ For more about saving things, see page 9.
▶ To enter info, see chapter 4.

The main Memos screen

If the current category is All, the main Memos screen lists all your memos. Open a memo, and then scroll through others by pressing right and left on the navigator. By default, memos are sorted chronologically. You can also manually arrange them (see next tip). To alphabetize memos, select **Options > Preferences** and tap **Alphabetic** from the pick list.

Organize your memos

Before a big meeting, categorize all the relevant memos and then put them in the order in which you'll need them. Touch a memo with your stylus and drag up or down. When you lift your stylus from the screen, the memo moves to where the dotted line is. To revert to the previous order, select **Options > Preferences** and choose the appropriate sorting method.

Brain-dump into memos

Each memo can hold the equivalent of about 2,500 words, or about six single-spaced typewritten pages.

Memo titles

The first line of your memo becomes its title. Phrase it in a way that'll help you remember what it contains.

Get Going → Chapter 11 → Memos →

Memos menus

Menus help you write, share, back up, and navigate your memos. Save time by entering long memos in Palm® Desktop software, and sync to create backups of your memos.

Quick new memos

In the list view, you don't have to tap New to get a new memo – just start writing in the input area.

Menu commands

$/n$ New memo

$/d$ Delete memo

$/c$ Copy

$/p$ Paste

$/s$ Select all

Go to

▶ To secure your memos, see page 34.

▶ To enter info into memos with Palm Desktop, see page 68.

Add phone numbers fast

To insert a name and phone number from Contacts into a memo, write the command $/\uparrow$ from within the memo. The Contacts list appears. Highlight the name you want and tap **Add**.

Cut and Paste

Open Palm Desktop on your computer, and simply cut and paste text from the Internet or an email into a new memo in Palm Desktop, then sync. This technique is perfect for directions, long lists, travel itineraries, and agendas.

Navigate Memos

		In Memos' list view, use the navigator to scroll through categories.
		Press the center key to select the first memo. Press center again to open the memo. Press left to deselect.
		After opening a memo, press left for the previous memo; press right for the next.

Memos menus

Record (entry view)

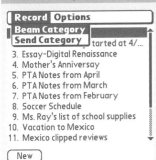

The Memos list view has two menus. Tap the **Record** menu to beam memo categories. Tap the **Options** menu to improve readability by changing the font of the memo list, and to set preferences and security levels.

Edit (entry view)

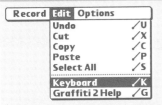

From within a memo, tap the **Edit** menu to transfer blocks of info in and out of the Memos application. Select **Keyboard** if you don't want to use Graffiti® 2 writing.

Options (entry view)

Change the font from within a memo. Use **Phone Lookup** to insert names and phone numbers of people in Contacts into a memo.

Use ShortCuts for faster Memos

ShortCuts can make creating memos faster. Predefined ShortCuts such as date and time stamps make it easy to quickly include the date and time you create your memo. Use custom ShortCuts to quickly enter phrases you use often. For more about ShortCuts, see page 42.

Attach a memo to a contact

Some of your memos might pertain to your contacts. Once you've written a memo, select **Edit > Select All > Copy**. Go to Contacts, open the entry you want, and tap **Record > Attach Note**. Then select **Edit > Paste**. Keep in mind that notes don't hold as much info as memos, so there are limits to how much you can include.

Share your favorites

Keep memo lists of your favorite books, movies, and restaurants, and beam them to your friends.

Documents To Go

Documents To Go is included on your installation CD. It's great for long memos, spreadsheets, and even presentations. See page 128.

Memos categories

Create or edit categories by selecting **Edit Categories** from the pick list.

Because memos can pertain to so many different areas of your life – work responsibilities, directions to the family picnic, study notes – you'll want to create plenty of categories to organize your information. To assign a category to a memo, open the memo, tap Details, and select a category name. Consider matching these categories up with the categories you use in other applications.

Mark important categories

Put a symbol such as a plus (+) or asterisk (*) before a category name to make it appear first on the category list.

Go to

▶ To learn more about categories, see page 24.

▶ To delete stuff, see page 26.

▶ To create ShortCuts, see page 42.

Naming memos

Establish conventions within a category for how you name memos. For instance, for a memo category called "Diary," start with the date, or in a category called "Recipes" start with "Soup," "Salad," or "Dessert." Remember that the first words of a memo become the title you see in list view.

Filing methods

If you take a lot of short memos and have trouble organizing them, begin each memo with a date/time stamp (ℓ**dts**). Or begin with a number such as 004 or 005, and file memos alphabetically by setting a filing preference in **Menu** > **Options** > **Preferences**.

Memo categories

Set exercise goals

Create a category called "Workouts." Make a memo titled "Goals, [current month]" with a list of your exercise goals for the month. Each month, copy and paste last month's text into a new memo, and write in your new goals. Now you can track your progress throughout the year.

Track job progress

Create a category called "Work Goals." Every week, create memos for each accomplishment. Write a few lines about what you did and the specific results. Before your performance review, send the memos to Word so you can create a self-evaluation to present to your boss (**Palm Desktop** > **Edit** > **Send To** > **MS Word**).

Taxes

Keep track of expenditures that might be deductible. An entry such as "building permit, $75, July 23rd," filed under the category of Taxes, might come in very handy come April 15th. In fact, a few memos like that might effectively pay for your handheld within a fiscal year or two.

Bright ideas

Create a catch-all category for memos to keep track of ideas, and then organize them later.

Merge, don't delete

When you want to get rid of a category but not its entries, rename the category with an existing category name. The entries will merge into that category.

Create memos within categories

Easily create new memos in a specific category by going to the list view for that category and tapping **New**. Cycle through categories while in the list view by pressing right on the navigator.

Samples of Memos categories

Parent	Artist	Small-business owner
Parent-teacher stuff	Art supplies	Urgent
Recipes	Ideas	Customer requests
Golf course reviews	Places to visit	Free time
Soccer field directions	Wines to try	Marketing ideas
Gifts	Exhibits to visit	Supplier issues
Vacation ideas	Restaurants to try	Conferences
Baby-sitter notes	Artists to investigate	Tax notes

More Memos techniques

Real Life Memos

Jerry's a frequent-flying consultant who always found airplane trays cramped, even for a small laptop. By adding a portable keyboard to his handheld, he created an ultracompact laptop substitute. Now he types documents in comfort and syncs after he lands.

Delete memos

To delete a memo, open the memo and select **Details** > **Delete**. Check the **Save archive copy on PC** box (unless you're sure you don't want to keep a backup) and tap **OK**.

Write long memos faster by using a portable keyboard or entering information in Palm Desktop software, and then sync. You can also cut and paste text from apps on your PC into Palm Desktop before synchronizing.

Don't format memos

You might be tempted to spruce up your memos with indents, bullets, or other formatting. Resist the urge. The memos won't retain such features. Instead, write in the plainest text possible and sync. In Palm Desktop, select **Edit** > **Send To** > **MS Word** and format in Word.

Print memos

You can use Palm Desktop software to print memos for handy reference or record-keeping. If you have a Mac, you can print to common day-calendar formats or create your own format. Palm Desktop software has lots of printing options. For details, see page 67.

☑ **Chapter 11: Did you discover how to...**

Title your memos so they don't get lost?... Attach a memo of music recommendations to a friend's contact info?... Use Palm Desktop for faster memos?... Think of five memo categories to create?... Share a list of favorite movies and restaurants?

Get Going → Chapter 12 →

Note Pad

Note Pad lets you quickly capture ideas and information in your own handwriting, such as phone numbers, thoughts, lists, and sketches. Note Pad is all about convenience and speed, but it also has some smart features worth learning.

In this chapter

▶ Sort your notes

▶ Change note colors

▶ Use reminder alarms with notes

Use the navigator

Note Pad lists notes the same way Memos lists memos. Press the center navigator button to select a note. Scroll through Note Pad by pressing right or left on the navigator or tapping the arrows at the top of the screen.

Change the pencil

In any note, tap the pencil icon to select one of three line widths, or use the eraser to erase part of a note you've written. In general, thin lines are better for longer notes. Use thick lines when you're writing a few quick words or drawing a simple figure.

Notes and Memos

People sometimes confuse Memos and Note Pad. The two applications share many features, but in Note Pad, the information you enter is preserved in your own handwriting. In Memos, the information you enter – via Graffiti® 2 writing or a keyboard – creates a typed memo.

Go to

▶ To attach notes to events and contacts, see page 44.

▶ To learn about Memos, see page 97.

Note Pad menus

Icon to look for

Note Pad

Note Pad lets you scribble notes and doodles, but it's more than the ultimate bar napkin. Because they're in your handwriting, notes are more personal and quicker than memos.

Organize Note Pad

From the list view, tap **Options** > **Preferences** and choose to sort manually. Now you can move notes around by tapping and dragging them.

Find notes on your computer

When you sync, your notes are transferred to Palm® Desktop software. Here you can view and delete your Note Pad's contents, but you can't print or add notes. On Macs, notes are filed in a separate application called Note Pad.

Notes vs. Memos

When to create a note? When to create a memo? If you need to jot down something short and quick, use Note Pad. If you're writing something descriptive that you may want to cut and paste, use Memos.

Track phone calls

Create a category in Note Pad called "Calls to Return." When you listen to your messages, jot down who called about what. Use the **Alarm** menu command (/a) and set an alarm to remind yourself to return the call.

Colorize your notes

From the Note Pad list screen, tap the **Menu** icon, open the **Options** menu, and select **Preferences** > **Color**. Change the paper to black and the pen color to yellow for arresting notes. This changes the color scheme of all your notes until you switch colors again.

The Record menu

Within a note, use the **Record** menu to create a new note, delete the current note, or beam a note. Commands, such as (/b) to beam a note, let you do all this faster.

Note Pad menus

Options (list view)

When you open Note Pad, it displays a screen on which you can take a new note. Tap **Done** to go to list view. Use the **Options** menu to change your preferences and security settings. In **Preferences**, you can sort alphabetically, by date, or manually. Manual sorting is especially useful because note titles automatically use the time and date as a default title. Select **Color** to change the color of the pen and the background.

Options (entry view)

Within a note, use the **Options** menu to change the font, set an alarm, change categories, or change the privacy setting. Tap **Alarm** to set the date and time for an alarm, or to turn the alarm off. In **Details**, mark the note as private and assign it a category.

Use the Edit menu

Change the title of a note by tapping the **Menu** icon and selecting the **Edit** menu. You can Undo, Cut, Copy, Paste, and Select All within the title of your note.

Create maps

If somebody needs simple directions to a restaurant or hotel, draw them a map on your handheld and then beam it to them.

Play games

Note Pad works great for Tic-Tac-Toe, Hangman, and Connect the Dots. Use it to pass the time with your friends or your kids.

Clear a note

You can clear a Note Pad screen without erasing every line. Tap the **Edit** menu and select **Clear Note**. To delete a note, open it and tap **Delete**.

Take it everywhere

Note Pad is another great reason to take your handheld everywhere. Leave those leaky pens and scraps of paper at home.

Menu commands

/a Alarm
/f Font
/n New note
/d Delete note

More Note Pad techniques

Real Life
Note Pad

Construction on Kate's dream house starts next month. When she visits the site, she sketches her basic floorplan notions in Note Pad to share with her architect, who lives 50 miles away. She syncs to her PC, opens Note Pad in Palm Desktop software, selects the note, and sends it to the architect. The next time they talk on the phone, her architect has a much clearer understanding of Kate's ideas.

Note Pad is great when you're on the go. Use it to keep track of things, but don't forget to have fun with it, too.

Transfer note ideas to memos

Create the same categories in Note Pad and Memos. When you're on the go, jot things down in Note Pad. Later, transfer ideas in Note Pad to the appropriate memos and add detail. The same technique works for Calendar, Contacts, and Tasks.

Get sketchy

Sometimes a crude sketch can express more than a phrase. Give it a try.

Quick contact info

On the run? Jot down a new acquaintance's name, phone, and email in Note Pad, and return later to enter the details in Contacts.

Use the alarm

Alarms in Note Pad are a great way to remember something you might otherwise forget. Create an alarm for a note by selecting **Options** > **Alarm**. Select the **Date** box to set the date and time for the alarm.

☑ **Chapter 12: Did you discover how to...**

Use notes and memos together?… Jot a note about a concert listing and set an alarm to remind yourself to buy tickets?… Use Note Pad as a simple phone memo system, complete with alarms?… Draw a map for getting to the airport?

Photos and music

Leave those ungainly photo albums and fading, dog-eared photos at home. Your handheld lets you see and share photos wherever you go. And RealOne® Mobile Player turns your handheld into a portable stereo. Transfer MP3 music files from your computer to an expansion card for listening at the gym or during your commute.

How many songs do cards hold?
Figures are for typical MP3s (recorded at 128 kbps).

Card size	Approximate capacity
64 MB	1 hour of music
128 MB	2 hours of music
256 MB	4 hours of music

In this chapter

▶ Manage digital photos on your handheld

▶ Edit photos in Palm® Desktop software

▶ Transfer MP3 files from your PC to your handheld

Expansion card required

You need an expansion card (sold separately) to listen to music on your handheld. Note that music and photos can reside on the same card.

Card reader

A must-have accessory for active MP3 or photo usage is a card reader that plugs into the USB port of your laptop or PC. A process that might take 20 minutes via sync requires only a few minutes with a card reader.

All about Photos

Your handheld lets you store, share, and view full-color digital photographs. Most pictures you've downloaded or taken with a digital camera are viewable directly on your handheld. In Windows, use Palm Desktop to create albums and slide shows to share with friends.

Install Photos

You must install Photos onto your handheld from the installation CD. Windows users, add photos to Palm Desktop and then sync them to your handheld. Mac users, add the Send To Handheld droplet to the Dock and then drag photos directly onto it from iPhoto.

Windows

If you have a Windows PC, use Palm Desktop to edit and view photos.

Mac

If you have a Mac, use iPhoto or another app to edit and view photos.

Copy photos to your handheld

Windows

From My Computer or Windows Explorer, select the photos you want to copy. Drag and drop them onto the Photos app within Palm Desktop. Synchronize.

Mac

Make the Send To Handheld droplet (in your palmOne folder) a permanent part of your desktop by dragging the droplet to the Dock. Drag photos onto the droplet and synchronize.

View, organize, and name photos

1 In the thumbnail or list view, tap a photo to display it. Tap it again to go back to the previous view. Tap the **Slide Show** button to watch a slide show; tap the screen to stop it.

2 In the list view, tap the **Name** header bar to switch between ascending and descending order. Tap **Date** to reverse the date order. Drag the divider to create more space.

3 Use the **Photo** menu to view photo details, delete or rotate photos, copy photos to an expansion card, and more. If you've installed SMS or email, Send Photo appears.

Four great uses for Photos

▶ Carry your pictures in digital photo albums instead of in your wallet.

▶ Use photos to create a pictorial catalog of something you're selling.

▶ Send or beam albums to friends, family, and peers.

▶ Carry photos of different stages of a do-it-yourself project for reference.

Icon to look for

Photos

See all photos

To see all photos on the handheld, in the upper-right corner, select **All Photos**. Go to the expansion card to see photos saved there.

Show slides

Tap **Slide Show** to display all the photos in the current album automatically, one after another. Tap a photo to stop the show.

Slide delay

Does the beauty of your photos need time to sink in? Tap the **Menu** icon and select **Options** > **Preferences** to set a delay of up to a full minute.

Photo file formats

Photos are saved in JPEG (JPG) format. On an expansion card, you can also save them in BMP, TIFF (uncompressed), and GIF formats.

Get Media → Chapter 13 → Photos →

Manage and share photos

Three ways to send and receive photos

▶ Save photos to an expansion card, and share the card.

▶ Beam photo files.

▶ Sync with your PC and email photos.

Edit photos on your computer to get them just right, and then synchronize to transfer them to your handheld. Now you can share them anytime, with anybody. By storing them on expansion cards, you can carry hundreds of photos on one slim handheld that's always with you.

Use the navigator

In the list or thumbnail view, press the center button to select a photo.

In the list view, press left to deselect; press right to go to Photo Details.

With a picture showing, press right or left to go to the next or previous one.

Direct photo viewing

If you have a digital camera that uses SD™ memory cards, you can slide a card into your handheld and show off your pictures on your handheld's larger screen.

Remove red-eye and crop photos

Click **Editor** in the Photos app in Palm Desktop to crop photos and remove red-eye. iPhoto for Mac has these features, too.

More freedom with photos

If you have a camera that uses SD expansion cards, you can take the card straight from the camera into your handheld for immediate, and much clearer, viewing. It's a great way to see which photos to delete on the camera. Sharing your photos can go far beyond just showing them off. If a friend or client has a palmOne handheld, you can easily beam photos to them.

Manage photos fast in Palm Desktop

Email	If email is enabled on your computer, select a photo; then click **E-mail** to send the photo from Palm Desktop.
Editor	Name your photos, crop them, adjust brightness, remove red-eye, and preview what the photo will look like on your handheld.
Photo details	Check size and resolution, and assign photos to albums. You can also add or read photo notes.
Zoom in or out	Use the magnifying glass at the lower left of the screen to zoom in and out of the photo when you want to see more detail.

Move photos to an expansion card

1 Insert an expansion card. Open **Photos** and tap the pick list in the upper-right corner.

2 Select an album and a photo. From the **Photo** menu, select **Copy to Card**.

Rotate big photos

If a hi-res photo takes too long to rotate on your handheld, rotate it in Palm Desktop before you synchronize it to your handheld.

Edit photos

The editing tools that come with Palm Desktop software can make you feel like a pro. Experiment with cropping, reducing red-eye, and adding text to touch up and salvage good shots with minor imperfections.

See photo details

On your handheld, from the list or thumbnail view, select **Photos** > **Details** to title a photo. This view is also available in Palm Desktop.

Sort photos

In the list view, tap **Name** to list photos in ascending order. Tap again to list in descending order. Tap **Date** to sort from oldest to most recent (or smallest to largest). Tap again to reverse the order.

Macs and photos

Mac users use iPhoto or another app, not Palm Desktop, to edit photos. Export pictures from iPhoto to the desktop, and then drag and drop them on the **Send To Handheld** droplet.

Listen to music

Icon to look for

RealOne

You don't need a separate MP3 player to listen to music on the go. Just sync your MP3 files from your computer to an expansion card, open RealOne Mobile Player on your handheld, and tap Play.

RealOne Player tips

▶ Background playback continues even when your handheld is in sleep mode.

▶ RealOne Mobile Player automatically stops after it plays the last song in a playlist (unless you hit the continuous play icon).

What's MP3?

MP3 has become the most common digital music file format because it delivers good sound with relatively small file sizes. Your handheld plays songs formatted in MP3.

Plug and play

Your handheld has a small speaker and a headphone jack. You can also plug amplified desktop computer speakers into the jack for a great stereo experience. All you need is an expansion card.

Watch your battery

The battery on your handheld drains more quickly when you're listening to music.

Go to

▶ To learn more about expansion cards, see pages 16 and 138.

Play music

Tap **Songs** to see a list of playable songs. Select **Playlist** to create a new list of songs you want to play or to edit an old one. Use the **Options** menu to get help.

Master your digital stereo controls

1 Title, Artist, Album	(lit when on)
2 Get info	7 Play/Pause
3 Time left/total length	8 Stop
4 Position slider	9 Go to previous song in list
5 Continuous play (lit when on)	10 Go to next song in list
6 Random order	

Continuous and random play

Use continuous play to loop endlessly through your songs until you tap **Stop**. Use random play to shuffle songs randomly. Look for the light to tell you which is on.

Changing songs

Use the position slider to move to a different place in a song. Simply touch it with your stylus and drag it. Tap the controls underneath the position slider to move to the next song, or to the previous one.

Turn it up

Tap the volume control and move the icon to the right for louder sound.

Where to store songs

Store songs on an expansion card (sold separately). You can switch cards anytime, even if your handheld is on.

Use the navigator

	Main screen	Songs screen
	Previous track	N/A
	Next track	N/A
	Volume up	Scroll song list up
	Volume down	Scroll song list down
	Play or pause	Select song

Be your own DJ

► Tap **Playlists** at the bottom of the RealOne Mobile Player screen to create and edit your playlists.

► Any song can be shared by multiple playlists.

► Start the playlist by tapping a song on the list.

Get Media → Chapter 13 → Photos →

Transfer music to your handheld

Real Life
Music

Marta listens to music on her handheld on the train, commuting to and from work. At home, she transfers a CD or two of music at a time from her computer to a 128 MB SD card, giving her more than enough music for the 80-minute commute. At work, she recharges her handheld. That way, she makes sure there's plenty of battery power for her to hum along all the way home.

Got a PC? Copy music from your CD collection to your computer using RealOne Player, and then sync songs directly from RealOne Player to your handheld. Got a Mac? Use music software such as iTunes to copy music, and then drag MP3 files to the Send To Handheld droplet and sync.

Transfer songs from a CD

RealOne help

Get help with RealOne Mobile Player at www.RealOne.com or through the Help menu of RealOne Player.

Windows

Use RealOne Player to transfer songs you copied from a CD. In your handheld's RealOne Mobile Player, tap **Menu > Options > Help** for details. Sync.

Mac

Use iTunes or other music software to create MP3 files. Drag them to the **Send To Handheld** icon, and sync them to your expansion card.

Transfer songs from your computer

If you already have MP3s on your computer, just drop them in **Quick Install** (Windows) or **Send To Handheld** (Mac). Sync to transfer music to your expansion card.

Fit more songs

Squeeze more songs onto an expansion card by compressing them. RealOne Player and iTunes both use a default rate of 128 kbps. In Preferences, change that to 64 kbps and you can fit twice as many songs. The music won't sound as great, but you can listen to more of it.

iTunes and your handheld

You can use iTunes to create MP3 files from CDs that you own, but at this time, songs from the iTunes Music Store will not transfer to your handheld. They are protected files that play only on computers with iTunes or on iPods.

What's bit rate?

Kilobits per second (kbps), or bit rate, is the measure of MP3 quality. CDs are recorded at about 1400 kbps. For handhelds, 128 kbps MP3 files are just fine, 96 kbps is comparable to FM broadcasts, and 64 kbps is like an AM broadcast.

CDs or downloads?

As you probably know, music buyers have a lot of options these days. It's up to you whether to download music directly from an online service or to buy CDs and copy files. The latter option does give you the benefit of album artwork and a CD for archiving.

"I'm a Little Teapot"

Nothing calms a noisy or impatient child like music. Keep an expansion card handy that's loaded with your kid's favorite songs. It's perfect for long trips in the car or airplane.

Charge in your car

The palmOne™ Mobility Kit allows you to power your handheld indefinitely with the cigarette lighter. To learn more about it (and other accessories), see page 140. You can also play your songs in your car by using a cassette or FM adapter – available at just about any electronics store – plugged into your handheld's headphone jack.

Get more help

Check out the Multimedia Handbook on *www.palmOne.com/support/tungstene* for details about how to get songs onto your handheld from your computer.

More music techniques

Make music

To perform music on your handheld, check the Internet for freeware and shareware programs that turn your handheld into an instrument, such as PocketSynth.

Listen to audio books

Both Windows and Mac users can listen to audio books, using Audible Player software. Windows users can install the Audible book player from the installation CD. Mac users need to go to Audible.com to download a player that works with iTunes and iSync. Once you join Audible.com, you'll be able to carry four or five complete books on a 128 MB expansion card.

Trouble transferring songs?

▶ Having trouble getting MP3s to sync to your handheld? Make sure you dragged your MP3s to Quick Install or the Send To Handheld droplet, and that you're synchronizing to a handheld with an expansion card in the slot.

▶ Having trouble synchronizing music from your PC's RealOne Player to your handheld? Answer these questions: Have you inserted an expansion card in your handheld? Is the card unlocked? Is RealOne Player open on both your PC and your handheld? Do you have songs queued up for transfer in the Palm Handheld window of RealOne Player? Is the green "Connected" light on in the lower-left corner?

Songs that skip

If a song skips during playback, the file is probably corrupted. Delete the song, sync with your computer, and try again.

More than music

You can transfer more than music to your handheld including periodicals, speeches, training classes, and more. Just make sure they're all in MP3 format.

☑ **Chapter 15: Did you discover how to...**

Choose the size of expansion card you'll need?... Play "Money Can't Buy Me Love" while you're working in Expense?... Create a playlist that lasts exactly as long as your workout?... Listen to your favorite mystery novelist on your handheld?

Get Cool Stuff → Chapter 14 →

Software

The Tungsten™ E comes preloaded with some great software, and you can easily transfer more good stuff from the installation CD. There's also great software at palmOne's website and at many, many other sites. This chapter discusses apps that are either already on your handheld or are included on your installation CD. To install them, insert the CD into your PC, follow the prompts, and then sync. On a Mac, drag the apps into the Install Handheld Files dialog box in Palm® Desktop, and then sync.

In this chapter

▶ Learn about the apps on your installation CD

Other free apps

Your handheld comes with lots of free software, some installed when you first sync, and others waiting on your CD for you to install. Windows users get Photos, Documents To Go, VersaMail®, Expense, and Calculator with the first sync they perform.

Not enough room

The apps on the CD not covered in this book are: Adobe Acrobat for Palm OS®, PowerOne Calculator, Handmark Magic Dogs, Telephony/ SMS, PhoneLink, Phone Link Updater, and Palm Dialer. Some of these are covered in the Tungsten E Handbook. See page xii.

Add software

For more information on how to add new software by synchronizing, see page 80.

Shop for Software

To buy new software, see page 132.

Get Cool Stuff → Chapter 14 → Software →

Application basics

Palm OS 5

Before you get a new app, make sure it works with Palm OS 5. Apps made for Pocket PC don't work with your handheld.

Compatibility

Some applications have features made expressly for different palmOne™ handhelds. For example some applications that say they work on palmOne Zire™ 72 handhelds won't work on your handheld.

If your handheld freezes

If your handheld freezes after you install a new application, check with the developer to see if the app supports Palm OS 5. To learn how to reset your handheld, see page 20.

As you explore the software that came on your installation CD and the 20,000-plus applications available for Palm OS® handhelds at www.palmOne.com/software (and elsewhere on the web), you'll find plenty of surprises.

Tailor-made interfaces

Applications such as MobileDB and RealOne® Player use the screen differently. In the middle of the screen, MobileDB uses lists. Tap to see another layer of detail. It also uses the footer for global commands. By contrast, the display for RealOne® Mobile Player mimics a CD player's buttons, but has menus and lists for organizing playlists. Explore how a new app works by checking the menus and tapping around.

Exploring applications

Application views

Many applications have a list view, a detail view, and a more detailed view of each entry. You drill down every time you tap something on the main part of the screen, and climb out by tapping icons or words at the bottom of the screen.

Where to find menus

No matter the app, you can open the menus by tapping the **Menu** icon in the lower-left corner of the input area.

Look for the manual

For third-party applications, check the vendor's web site for an online manual.

Find your way back

If you ever find yourself lost in a detail screen of a detail screen of a detail screen, tap the **Home** icon. You'll never lose information on any Palm OS app.

Find software

Buy software at any computer or office supply store or from one of the many online retailers, including www.palmOne. com/software. Many applications have trial versions that let you pay later, after you've decided whether the app is right for you.

Keep apps on your handheld

In general, keep applications on your handheld and files on an expansion card. Many apps stored on an expansion card work fine, but if you have an app on a card and swap the card, you lose access to the app.

Application tips

► If an application won't transfer when you sync, your handheld or card may be full, or the app may be incompatible with your handheld.

► If you can't find your new app after synchronizing, check the **Unfiled** category from the Home screen.

► As a precaution, take time to sync before you install a new app. That way, you'll have a backup on your computer if you run into problems with installation.

► If you delete an app without deleting the backup on your computer, it may keep coming back every time you sync. Be sure to delete troublesome apps (and utilities) from both the handheld and the computer, and then sync.

Go to

► To learn how to transfer apps to your handheld, see page 80.

► To explore software available at www.palmOne.com/ software, see page 133.

Expense

Icon to look for

Expense

Expense makes it easy to keep track of what you spend. Use it to record business travel, hobby income, or just to keep track of your weekly budget.

Use with Palm Desktop

Expense is automatically backed up on Palm Desktop every time you sync. Add, delete, and organize your expenses on your PC, and then sync back to your handheld.

See where your money goes

If you don't use Quicken or Money to track your finances, but you're curious about where the paycheck goes, Expense is a great way to find out. Use Expense for a month – record everything, right down to quarters that go into vending machines – and export to Excel at month's end for an eye-opening portrait of your spending habits.

Enter expenses fast

When you enter a new expense, your handheld defaults to today's date. If you're entering expenses as you make them, you can skip the step of entering the date.

Add notes

Add a note in Receipt Details if you think you might forget the reason for an expense.

Send expenses to Excel

1 Sync with your PC. Info from Expense is backed up in Palm® Desktop software.

2 In Palm Desktop, click **Expense**. Select the entries and click **Edit** > **Send To** > **MS Excel**.

Create an expense

1 Tap **New** to create a new expense. A new entry pops up with the current date. Tap the **Expense type** pick list and select a type. Then enter the amount.

Expense		▼ All
3/2 Breakfast	$	11.00
3/2 Bus	$	1.00
3/2 Car Rental	$	75.00
3/2 Entertainment	$	8.50
3/2 Snack	$	4.00
3/2 -Expense type-	$	

(New) (Details...) (Show...)

2 Select an entry and tap **Details**. Select a **Category**, reclassify the **Type** of expense, and record how and whom you paid.

Receipt Details

Category: ▼ Unfiled
Type: ▼ Breakfast
Payment: ▼ Cash
Currency: ▼ $
Vendor: |
City:
Attendees: Who...

(OK) (Cancel) (Delete) (Note)

3 The Show Options box pops up when you tap **Show**. Choose how to sort your expenses, whether or not to show currency, and how to record distance.

Expense		▼ All
3/2 Breakfast	$	11.00
3/2 Bus	$	1.00
3/2 Car Rental	$	75.00

Show Options ℹ

Sort by: ▼ Date

Distance: Miles / Kilometers

☑ Show currency

(OK) (Cancel)

Change the default currency

When traveling abroad, change your default currency by selecting **Options > Preferences > Default Currency**.

Quick summary

To quickly see how much you spent in any type of expense, customize your view to sort by type. Similar transactions are grouped together.

Change your view

By default, Expense sorts chronologically. To sort in another way, tap the **Show** button and select from the pick lists.

SplashMoney

Icon to look for

Use SplashMoney – included on your installation CD – to manage your bank accounts, credit cards, assets, and liabilities, or just to keep yourself within your monthly budget.

A.K.A. PDA Money

To install SplashMoney, click **PDA Money** on your installation CD. (On some Tungsten E handhelds, SplashMoney appears as PDA Money.)

Sync with Quicken

If you buy a special conduit, you can sync SplashMoney directly to Quicken, Microsoft Money, or Excel. For info, see www.splashdata.com/splashmoney.

Go to

▶ The SplashMoney User Guide on your installation CD is full of useful tips.

Open it quickly

If you use SplashMoney often, set an application button to open it. Select **Home > Prefs > Buttons**.

Password protection

Password-protect info in SplashMoney by going to **Options > Set Password**.

What you can do with SplashMoney

▶ Keep tabs on your checking, savings, and other accounts.

▶ Monitor credit card purchases and payments.

▶ Stay on target with your weekly, monthly, or yearly budget.

▶ Manage home improvement projects.

▶ View reports by month, quarter, current year, or previous year.

▶ Enter an expense or ATM debit on the spot.

Using SplashMoney

Register View

▶ Tap the **Accounts** list to toggle accounts.

▶ Tap a transaction to edit it.

▶ Tap the column heading to sort transactions.

Use symbols to identify accounts

Assign symbols to new accounts to quickly distinguish them from others. Create an account and tap the **Icon** box. Select from 63 symbols, ranging from a mobile phone to a heart.

Distinguish between accounts

If you have multiple accounts, it can be hard to keep them straight. Color-code them in Register View by selecting **Options** > **Choose Row Color** or **Choose Header Color**.

Balance menu

▶ Displays the Ending Balance, the amount typically recorded in your checkbook register.

▶ Displays Cleared Balance, the amount that has cleared your bank.

Organize using accounts

In SplashMoney, your account list is in the upper-right corner. It's easy to toggle between accounts. Payees, categories, and classes you create are auto-filled the next time you try to complete them.

Financial reports

Use SplashMoney to create reports and budgets. Select an account. From the menu, select **Reports and Budgets**.

Real Life SplashMoney

Jimmy takes business trips to Asia that often last for weeks. It's easy for him to lose track of spending, so he uses SplashMoney to periodically create reports that monitor his progress. The currency converter lets him quickly understand the percentage of his budget he's spent, so he doesn't have to mentally switch between dollars and yen (and sometimes other currency). Before the trip ends, he can tell whether he's been frugal. If he has been, he rewards himself with a spectacular meal before returning home.

Set preferences

▶ Select **Options** > **Preferences** to choose which categories to show and whether to show the year for transactions.

▶ To decrease the size of the font to display more information, select **Options** > **Font**.

Get Cool Stuff → Chapter 14 → Software →

Palm Reader

Icon to look for

PalmReader

New name

As this book was going to press, Palm Reader changed hands. It is now called eReader, but the version on your CD is still called Palm Reader. Download books at palmOne's eBook Store, which has over 12,000 titles under $10. Upgrade to eReader Pro to get advanced display options.

Audio books

Go to Audible.com and you'll find audio books to download to your handheld. The software is free and the audio books are sold separately, or by a monthly subscription. Audible software works with both Windows PCs and Macs.

Use Palm® Reader to read ebooks wherever you go, without weighing yourself down. Bookmark pages, search for significant lines or words, and even attach notes. Ebooks are surprisingly readable on your handheld. Download titles from http://ebooks.palmone.com.

Preferences and tools

Preferences

Select **Menu** > **Options** for a full set of preferences, plus Auto-scrolling. Turn the page by pressing down or right on the navigator.

Book tools

The toolbar performs the same functions as a menu. Choose which toolbar icons to show in **Options** > **Toolbar Preferences**.

Bookmarks and notes in books

1 Press the center navigator button to bookmark a page. To name a bookmark, select **Go > Add Bookmark**. Go to the bookmarks list (right) by tapping the bookmark icon.

2 From any page, create a note by selecting **Go > Add Note** (/n). To see all your notes within the book (shown here), tap the **Note** icon at the bottom of any page.

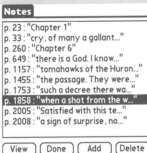

Find key passages

Impress your classmates by instantly searching out key words and phrases. Use the Find command (/f) to move around books fast.

Take notes

Take notes as you read (tap **Menu > Go > Notes**), and then export them into a memo you can print from Palm Desktop. Select **Menu > Book > Export Notes**, and then sync.

Where to get ebooks

Download ebooks and sync them to your handheld. Below are a few good sites for starting your library.

▶ http://ebooks.palmone.com

▶ www.ebookmall.com/palm

▶ www.powells.com/ebookstore/palmreader.html

▶ http://etext.lib.virginia.edu/ebooks

Learn to use the toolbar icons

The toolbar icons in Palm Reader make it easy to bookmark pages, take notes, and even switch between books. Practice with them to speed up and enrich reading and studying.

Leave heavy books behind

Palm Reader lets you leave more books at home. It's great for students who don't want to lug heavy backpacks, and for commuters who'd rather keep their briefcases thin.

Palm Reader tips

▶ Adjust brightness for easier reading by tapping the **Brightness** icon in the writing area.

▶ To improve readability, use the **Options** menu to change the text size or invert the screen.

▶ Create and assign categories for all your books by opening a book and tapping the **Info** icon at the bottom of the page.

▶ Change the display to horizontal in **Options > Screen Preferences**.

Get Cool Stuff → Chapter 14 → Software →

MobileDB

Icon to look for

MobileDB

If you're familiar with databases, you'll find MobileDB a nimble way to manage large amounts of unwieldy info. Use it to create new lists and databases, revise existing ones, and manage long lists. The databases come premade and you can get new ones online.

What you can do with MobileDB

▶ Track complex information, such as who contributed, when they contributed, and how much they contributed to your fund-raising triathlon this year, last year, and the year before.

▶ Create individual entries for each of your company's products.

▶ Export databases to Contacts or Calendar.

Learn more

Learn how to create, print, and synchronize new databases at www.mobiledb.com.

Using MobileDB

1   From the list view of MobileDB, you see the list of available databases. Edit and assign categories in the upper right. Create new databases in the lower left.

2   Tap a database to open it.

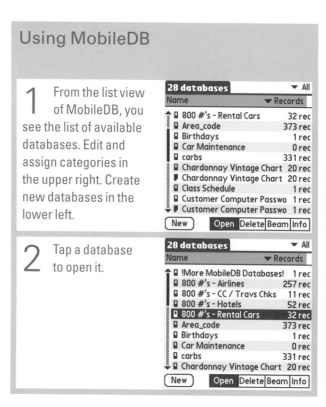

MobileDB techniques

Technique	How to do it
Improve legibility with color headers and alternating color rows	Select **Options** > **MobileDB Colors** or **Options** > **Colors**
Narrow the number of entries shown in a list	Select **Record** > **Filter** and enter the parameters you want
See all the entries of a database	Select **Record** > **Show All**
Sort entries by a field name	Tap a field name in the header
Make a modified version of a downloaded database	Select **Database** > **Clone**
Sort a database by multiple criteria	Select **Record** > **Sort**
Export entries to Calendar or Contacts	Select **Record** > **Export to Calendar** or **Record** > **Export to Contacts**
Export databases to Calendar or Contacts	Select **Database** > **Export to Calendar** or **Database** > **Export to Contacts**

Move around in MobileDB

To highlight a database entry, press the center navigator button. To scroll up or down the database list, press up or down on the navigator. To scroll through an entry's fields, press right or left.

Assign a password

Password-protect individual databases without protecting the whole program. Open the database and select **Database** > **Password**. Note that if you sync, the info won't be secure on your computer.

Real Life MobileDB

Marisa makes soundtracks for movies. She owns thousands of CDs and buys more every week. She uses one of the predefined database templates in MobileDB and customizes it to track her music purchases. At the record store, she looks up song and album titles to make sure she never buys anything she already owns.

MobileDB tips

▶ Use the navigator to scroll up or down a database ten entries at a time.

▶ A data field can contain up to 1,000 characters. A database can have up to 20 fields.

▶ Tap and drag the lines in the header of a database to adjust the width. Sometimes you can squeeze more into view.

Documents To Go

Icon to look for

Documents

Use Documents To Go Standard Edition, by DataViz, on your handheld to read and edit files compatible with Word and Excel. Transfer documents from your PC, write reports and edit spreadsheets, and then sync them to your PC to print, edit, and email – with most of the formatting still intact.

Things you can do with Documents To Go

▶ Keep important and dynamic documents up-to-date, such as project spreadsheets in Excel or memos written in Word.

▶ Beam and receive files to and from other handhelds and laptops.

▶ Edit documents during a flight and email them when you land.

Manual included

The manual for Documents To Go is included in the Help menu when you open Documents To Go on your computer.

Open in Windows

Open Palm Desktop and click the **Documents** icon to open Documents To Go in a separate window.

Open on a Mac

On Macs, Documents To Go is a separate application in your Applications folder.

The main screen

On your handheld, the main screen for Documents To Go is a list of the files managed by the application. Sort by tapping the column headings. Tap the page icons along the far left for a pick list of actions such as Delete, Beam, and Details.

Create a new document

1 On your handheld's Home screen, tap **Documents**, and then tap **New**.

2 Select a format. Files saved in Word or Excel format can be emailed to people who don't have Documents To Go.

Joe made an Excel spreadsheet to keep score at his son's high school baseball games. He used to print out a sheet, write on it, and enter the data when he got back home. Now he follows the game on his handheld, syncs when he gets home, and emails the spreadsheet to the other parents.

Sync

Changes to files are transferred when you sync, and retain much of the original formatting.

Save time

Have a big file you only need to sync occasionally? In the main Documents To Go view, if a column contains a small HotSync icon, that file will be synchronized. If a dash appears, it won't. Tap to toggle between the two.

Create reports and spreadsheets

Use Word and Excel formats to create files compatible with Word and Excel. People you share them with can open them in Word or Excel on their computer. The Word To Go and Sheet To Go formats create files that take up less space on your handheld, but they can be read only by people who also have Documents To Go. To change the file format, tap **Details.**

Add, store, share

▶ To add files, click the **Plus** icon at the top of the Documents To Go screen on your PC.

▶ Copies of files created on your handheld and synchronized using Documents To Go are stored in your My Documents folder (Windows) or Documents (Mac).

Get Cool Stuff → Chapter 17 → Software →

VersaMail®

VersaMail® personal email software lets you manage email on your handheld by synchronizing your handheld to your Windows PC. Keep your email with you for reference at meetings or for reading during a commute. Or write emails on the train and send when you get to the office.

Managing your email

You can buy wireless add-ons for your Tungsten E handheld (such as a Bluetooth adapter), but it's much simpler to sync with your PC so you can review your email while you're on the go. When you're back at home or in the office, sync again to transfer the changes to your PC. These pages assume you'll be synchronizing email with your handheld, not connecting wirelessly while mobile.

Read the Handbook

Get all the details for setup in the Tungsten E Handbook. The Handbook's many pages of details will guide you through setup and show you how to use all the features of VersaMail. See page xii for more info.

Save attachments to a card

Expansion cards have plenty of room for email attachments. When you open a new message, tap the red paper clip icon, and then tap **Save To Card**. Take your email with you and work offline.

Navigate VersaMail

 Select a message with the center navigator button. Press right to reveal a menu that lets you move messages, mark them as read or unread, reply, forward, or delete. Press up or down to scroll.

Set up a VersaMail account

1 Open VersaMail. Select **Menu** > **Accounts** > **Account Setup** (/ພ).

2 Tap **New** to begin setup. Tap the **Next** button until you've filled in all the prompts.

Customize VersaMail

1 Select **Options** > **Preferences**. Unless you have no other way to use email, leave **Delete Msgs on Server** unchecked.

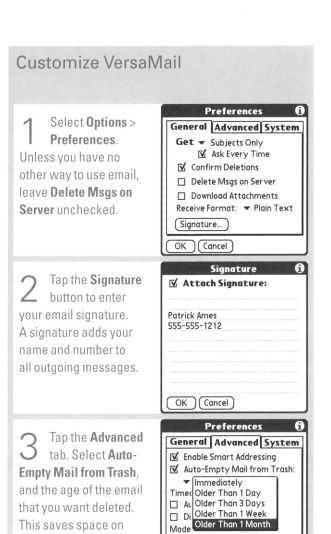

2 Tap the **Signature** button to enter your email signature. A signature adds your name and number to all outgoing messages.

3 Tap the **Advanced** tab. Select **Auto-Empty Mail from Trash**, and the age of the email that you want deleted. This saves space on your handheld.

Create documents

Use VersaMail to attach and send files you create in Documents To Go. Be sure you save the files in Word or Excel format, not Word To Go or Sheet To Go, because your recipient may not have Documents To Go.

Icon to look for

VersaMail

Email tips

▶ Create email filters to automatically sort your email into folders. Tap **Menu** > **Options** > **Filters**.

▶ Pick a font, style, and size that's easy to read. Tap **Menu** > **Options** > **Display Options**.

▶ As with email on your PC, you can attach a file on your handheld to an outgoing VersaMail message, including a Word document or Excel spreadsheet from Documents To Go.

Set up multiple accounts

Create multiple email accounts to receive, read, and send email to and from your different work and personal accounts.

Customize emails

Use different colors for read and unread emails, choose to show one or two lines of text, and select a sort order for emails. Tap the **Menu** icon and select **Options** > **Display Options**.

Get Cool Stuff → Chapter 14 → Software →

Shop for software

New apps pop up every day

Palm OS has some 50,000 registered developers. About 20,000 applications are currently available for Palm OS handhelds.

Troubleshooting

Some third-party applications can slow performance, freeze your handheld, or cause synchronizing problems if they're not compatible with your Tungsten E handheld. If your handheld freezes, delete your third-party applications. Reinstall and test them one at a time until you find the culprit. Remember to delete them from the backup files on your computer, too.

Go to

▶ To learn how to add software to your handheld, see page 80.

Your handheld is loaded with stuff, but thousands of third-party applications can make it even more powerful. These applications can do everything from helping you stay in shape to improving your productivity. Many are free to try before you buy.

Application types

Commercial

Buy commercial apps at www.palmOne.com/software, other retail stores, or other sites. They tend to perform important functions and have more powerful features.

Shareware

Shareware apps typically do smaller things. They usually offer trial runs that eventually make you pay.

Freeware

You can download thousands of programs for free, from productivity tools to games. Some might crash your handheld, so read user comments before you install.

Visit Software Connection

At www.palmOne.com/software, you'll find thousands of applications divided into easy-to-use categories such as business and professional, games, personal productivity, and travel.

Click a section to get a list of software. Here, the Travel Software section is divided so you can check out a featured product, click the best-sellers, explore new titles, or browse for software in a variety of categories.

Click an application to get more detail about it. Find user ratings, how many others have downloaded it, and similar apps that might better suit your needs.

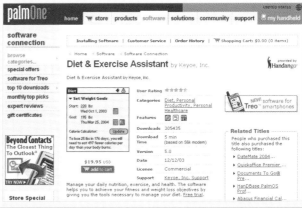

top 10 downloads
monthly top picks

Look for Software Connection's top 10 downloads and monthly picks to find popular and effective apps.

Fun and games

Solitaire

Your handheld's installation CD comes with a solitaire game.

Search the web for card games, handheld versions of old-school arcade games, and other fun apps.

Best picks

Atari Retro	Classic arcade games like Asteroids and Pong
Merriam-Webster Crossword Puzzles	Word games, plus 1,000 crossword puzzles
SimCity	Build cities and govern them as they grow
Scrabble	Play friends or the computer
Freeware (available at www.palmgear.com)	
Open Chess	Surprisingly good chess app
Wormy	Wormy grows with every cookie
HandyShopper	For shopping lists and more
SkyChart	Enter coordinates to study the night sky

☑ **Chapter 17: Did you discover how to...**

Keep tabs on your bank accounts in SplashMoney?... Officially stick your partner with the check again?... Download *The Brothers Karamazov* and share it with the brothers Mankiewicz?... Track down the people who didn't buy Girl Scout cookies this year?

Get Cool Stuff → Chapter 15 →

Accessories

From cases and covers to travel chargers and portable keyboards, accessories enhance and protect your handheld. New ones are introduced all the time – keep an eye on www.palmOne.com/store for the latest. To protect your handheld, consider an extended warranty plan as well.

Why get an extended warranty?

The palmOne™ Care plan

This is the best value when your warranty expires. For $49.95 ,you get a year of extended warranty coverage, two years of phone support, and a one-time free screen replacement.

Advance Exchange

Under normal warranty conditions, you send your broken handheld in to be repaired, and palmOne sends you back a fixed handheld. With Advance Exchange, available for $40, palmOne sends you a new device before fixing your broken one. The palmOne Care plan waives the fee altogether – you get a replacement handheld within three business days with no additional shipping charges.

In this chapter

► Learn about palmOne accessories

Phone support

You get 90 days of free telephone support. After that, phone support is $25 per call or $44.99 per year. Under palmOne Care, telephone support is included at no charge.

Warranty facts

► Your Tungsten™ E handheld has a 90-day warranty beginning on the day of purchase. Extend your warranty before it expires.

► Your warranty does not cover screen replacement.

► In the United States, you get phone support within 90 days of purchasing a palmOne handheld.

► Read about the extended warranty's terms and conditions at www.palmOne.com/support.

Cases and covers

Case and cover tips

► Two Graffiti® 2 stickers were included with your handheld. Stick them inside your case for quick reference.

► Keep losing your stylus? Buy a pack of extras at www.palmOne.com/store and tuck them in your case.

► Ultra-thin transparent screen protectors reduce glare and protect against scratches. They work best if you change them about once a month.

► Make sure the case isn't too small for your handheld. Check the specs on the package for compatibility with your model.

► Look for explicit mention of the Tungsten E handheld in the case description.

► Want color? palmOne persona cases come in a variety of colors.

No case can protect your handheld against every accident, but a case can greatly reduce the odds of scratches and other damage. Some cases have storage pouches for expansion cards, stylus replacements, and other stuff. If it's style you want, go to www.palmOne.com/persona and visit the line of specialty cases from Vaja.

What to look for in a case

Protection

A case that covers the screen is essential, but the rest of the handheld is also worth protecting. A hard case can protect the handheld from inevitable drops.

Storage

Many cases can store expansion cards, accessories, and a few personal items. Consider spending a few bucks more for a case that can replace your wallet.

Access

Cases that open and close with one hand are especially convenient. Also consider access to the sides and top of the handheld for headphones, power cords, and cables.

Types of cases (not all may be presently available)

	Materials	Pros	Cons
Soft case	Cloth or moisture-repellent fabric.	Covers screen, prevents scratches. May have space for cards and more.	Zippered. May slow down access to the handheld and muffle alarms and alerts.
Hard case	Plastic or aluminum hard shell.	Impact protection. May have spring-loaded access and storage.	May slow down access to the handheld and muffle alarms and alerts.
Leather case	Black or brown leather.	Holds handheld, extras, and wallet items such as credit cards in a functional package.	Some models still require screen protectors because the screen is constantly exposed.
palmOne persona	Stylish handsewn leathers.	Holds handheld, credit cards, expansion cards, and spare stylus. Can be engraved with your name, too.	If you don't mind the extra costs, these cases combine stylish form plus great functionality.

Expansion cards

Expansion card tips

▶ Buy a case that includes expansion card storage slots.

▶ Expansion cards are hot-swappable, which means you can eject or insert new cards any time the card is not in use.

▶ SD expansion cards have a small locking tab on the side. Move it down to lock the card, preventing any changes.

Once you discover that you can carry MP3 files, software, lots of photos, audio books, videos, and even complete movies on your handheld, an expansion card becomes a necessity. Buy a high-capacity card to hold everything (at least for a while), or a few smaller ones if you want to keep different categories of things separate. Keep the dummy card in a safe place and use it when a card is not present.

Suggested expansion card usages

Size	Comments	Usages
128MB	For light users, one card can cover everything	Holds your photos, a few audio books, and your extra files and apps.
256MB	Better for music use, audio book use, or lots of video	Holds everything you need for most average users, including 2 hours of music.
512MB	One card for all your needs	No worries about keeping track of multiple expansion cards.
1GB	Carry it all	Carry large segments of your office or your media plus over 8 hours of MP3s.

Software on cards and on CDs
Find a great selection at www.palmOne.com/store

Reference

The Britannica Concise Encyclopedia has more than 24,000 entries supported by more than 900 photos, maps, tables, and illustrations. Merriam-Webster's Collegiate Dictionary & Franklin Thesaurus contains more than 215,000 definitions and more than 340,000 synonyms and antonyms.

Games

The best selling NFL video game is now available for the first time ever for PDAs and mobile phones. Madden NFL 2005 provides the latest player stats and team line-ups and is completely updated for the 2004-2005 season. Playoffs, regular season, and exhibition game modes are all tracked with updated game stats.

Software on CD

Many games, references, and utility software are sold on CDs and copied to your PC. Then transfer what you want, when you need it, to an expansion card for use. The *Zondervan NIV Study Bible* is one popular example. Others include Centipede & More Classic Games, Directions on-the-go, and more. See www.palmOne.com for all the latest software on CDs you can transfer to your Treo smartphone.

Card readers

Buy a USB expansion card reader if you are serious about music, video, or photos. Shop for card readers that plug into the USB port of your computer and whose drivers are built in.

Backup

You can back up your entire handheld either fully or incrementally to an expansion card. Use software such as BackupMan, Bachmann's Mobile Backup, or Backup Buddy.

Card tip

When using a card reader on your desktop computer, make sure to eject the drive before removing the card. Files may be missing if you neglect to do this.

More accessories

Do more faster by adding accessories like portable keyboards, travel chargers, MP3 kits, cables, and other add-ons.

Where to buy

▶ One great place to get authorized accessories is www.palmOne.com. For a list of retailers, both online and in your city, see www. palmOne.com/wheretobuy.

▶ In Europe, visit www.palmdirect.com to buy palmOne products.

▶ In Australia, Malaysia, and Singapore, visit www.apacstore. palmOne.com.

▶ In Canada, visit http://canadastore. palmOne.com.

▶ Retail palmOne stores have all the newest accessories. For locations, see www.palmOne.com.

Stylus options

Why a stylus?

Your handheld's screen is touch-sensitive. It needs a semi-soft instrument to recognize your taps and handwriting. Never tap it with anything hard or metallic.

Replacements

Buy a replacement stylus for your Tungsten E handheld from www.palmOne.com/store (three for about five bucks). Any kind of stylus that doesn't fit your case or handheld is much more likely to get lost.

Bells and whistles

Alternatives include a pen-size stylus and other models equipped with laser pointers, flashlights, and hidden pens. There's even a 24-carat gold-plated stylus for most handhelds.

The Universal Wireless Keyboard

True portability

The Universal Wireless Keyboard from palmOne folds down to about the size of your handheld. It connects to your handheld via the IR port. It uses two AAA batteries and requires you to install a driver on your handheld.

Features

Full-size keys let you type fast, while special function keys enable tapping and stylus movements.

Compatibility

This keyboard works with your Tungsten E handheld and many other palmOne models as well.

Mini-USB

Your handheld has a mini-USB port for synchronizing and a power cable for charging.

Compatibility

Look for third-party products that support the Tungsten E handheld specifically. If a product doesn't list your handheld model as being compatible, don't buy it.

Use a wireless keyboard

In the back of a classroom or with downtime on the train, the palmOne Universal Wireless Keyboard is perfect for tasks that involve entering large amounts of info, like writing long emails or taking notes.

Audible books

A great use for your handheld is listening to audio books. Go to www.Audible.com to download software and books. Hook your car stereo to your handheld's headphone jack via a vehicle stereo connecting kit (sold separately at audio stores).

Power on the road

The palmOne™ Mobility Kit can charge your handheld from a car's cigarette lighter, and the included USB cable lets you sync while you're on the road. The Travel Charger includes plug adapters that work in most countries around the world.

Travel with your handheld

International power

Make sure you bring the Travel Charger. It includes interchangeable plug adapters that work in most electrical systems around the world.

Music and photos

Pack a couple of expansion cards with your favorite tunes so you'll have something to listen to while in transit. Pack a couple more for photos you'll take on your Tungsten E handheld.

Translators

Translator apps available at www.palmOne.com/software will help you get by in almost any language.

Your handheld makes a great travel companion. Try these ideas.

Get ready to travel – and then go!

Tasks
Make a to-do list before you leave.

Calendar
Attach notes to travel dates. Include frequent flyer and reservation numbers and other important travel info.

Contacts
Create a category for emergency contacts, and another with the people you'll call on your trip.

World Clock
Set your time zone and alarm so you don't miss your flights.

City maps and guides
Find maps and guides to hundreds of cities at www.palmOne.com/software.

☑ **Chapter 18: Did you discover how to...**

Find a carrying case that lets you toss your wallet?... Use an encyclopedia to answer "23 down, 'Hitchcock classic,' seven letters, starts with a V?"... Protect sensitive stuff on an SD expansion card?... Use a keyboard to write a new chapter every commute?

Glossary

application A software program you use for a specific purpose. Some apps are built in to your handheld, such as Calendar and Tasks. Others are included on your installation CD, and still others are available for purchase and/or download.

application buttons Buttons on the lower part of your handheld, each of which opens one of your handheld's applications. The Tungsten E handheld has buttons for Calendar, Contacts, Tasks, and Note Pad.

beam To transmit information to another device through your handheld's infrared port.

command An action you execute on your handheld, such as beaming an entry, deleting an application, or calling up a particular screen. Also see *command stroke* and *menu*.

command stroke A diagonal stroke made with the stylus, from the lower left to the upper right of the writing area. The command stroke by itself brings up the command toolbar, where you can tap icons to execute commands. The stroke followed quickly by a letter performs a command ($/c$ for copy, $/i$ for information). See *Graffiti® 2 writing*.

conduit A small program that specifies how (and whether) info is exchanged between your computer and your handheld. Each application has its own conduit, which is listed in the HotSync Custom dialog box.

enter To input information in any application on your handheld by typing or writing.

entry An individual set of information within an application, such as an event in Calendar or a person's contact information in Contacts. Also called a record.

expansion card A stamp-sized storage device that you insert into the slot at the top of your handheld. Expansion cards hold applications, songs, videos, pictures, and other information.

field A box where you enter information, such as an email address in Contacts or an event description in Calendar.

Graffiti® 2 writing The method that enables you to enter information and execute commands by writing with your stylus. Also see *command stroke* and *writing area*.

Home screen The main screen on your handheld, where you have access to all of your applications. To get there, tap the Home icon to the left of the writing area or hold down the center navigator button.

HotSync® process See *sync, synchronize*.

input area See *writing area*.

menu Lists of actions you can perform within an application. Use menus to edit information, set preferences, save, delete, beam, and more. In most applications, menus are hidden at the top of the screen. You make them visible by tapping the upper-left corner of the screen or the Menu icon, to the lower left of the writing area.

navigator The navigator, or five-way navigator, consists of the two large, concentric buttons in the middle of the lower part of your handheld. Press the edges to move up, down, right, or left, and the center button to select items. The navigator works differently in different applications, but it's usually an easy way to move around with one hand.

onscreen keyboard A small, standard keyboard that appears on the screen when you call it up by tapping ABC in the writing area. Tap the keyboard with your stylus to type.

Palm® Desktop software The means by which your computer shares information and applications with your handheld. It also lets you enter and edit information on your computer and then transfer it to your handheld. It is installed on your computer from the installation CD, and is often called Palm Desktop. Also see *sync, synchronize.*

Palm OS® The operating system, or basic underlying software, that your handheld uses. Your Palm OS is version 5.2.

pick list A list of choices found in many applications. See the choices by tapping a downward arrow.

record See *entry.*

screen The display area of a handheld. The entire screen is touch-sensitive and responds to tapping or drawing by the stylus. *Screen* can also refer to a particular place within an application, such as the Contact Edit screen in Contacts.

sync, synchronize To exchange and update information on your handheld and computer, so that your information is the same in both places. You synchronize also to transfer applications to your handheld. Also see *Palm® Desktop software.*

tap To touch the screen with your stylus to make something happen on your handheld.

view A particular way an application displays information. Calendar, for example, has Day View, Week View, Month View, and Agenda View. Many applications have a list view that shows you many entries at a glance.

writing area The area on your handheld below the display section of your screen, where you write letters and execute commands with your stylus. Also called the input area. Also see *Graffiti® 2 writing.*

Index

palmOne Pays Back program

Earn Rewards.

Enroll now in the palmOne
Pays Back program. Earn
palmOne gear, plus other
rewards from top online
retailers like the Palm Store,
Amazon, United® and more.
Joining palmOne Pays Back
is fun, easy and rewarding.
Simply tell your friends
about new palmOne prod-
ucts and you'll earn great
prizes when they make a
qualifying purchase.

isit Peachpit on the Web
t www.peachpit.com

- Read the latest articles and download timesaving tipsheets from best-selling authors such as Scott Kelby, Robin Williams, Lynda Weinman, Ted Landau, and more!

- Join the Peachpit Club and save 25% off all your online purchases at peachpit.com every time you shop—plus enjoy free UPS ground shipping within the United States.

- Search through our entire collection of new and upcoming titles by author, ISBN, title, or topic. There's no easier way to find just the book you need.

- Sign up for newsletters offering special Peachpit savings and new book announcements so you're always the first to know about our newest books and killer deals.

- Did you know that Peachpit also publishes books by Apple, New Riders, Adobe Press, Macromedia Press, palmOne Press, and TechTV press? Swing by the Peachpit family section of the site and learn about all our partners and series.

- Got a great idea for a book? Check out our About section to find out how to submit a proposal. You could write our next best-seller!

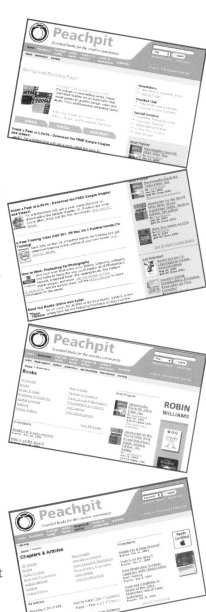